# Getting Started with TensorFlow

Get up and running with the latest numerical computing library by Google and dive deeper into your data!

**Giancarlo Zaccone**

PUBLISHING

BIRMINGHAM - MUMBAI

# Getting Started with TensorFlow

First published: July 2016

Production reference: 1190716

Published by Packt Publishing Ltd.
Livery Place
35 Livery Street
Birmingham
B3 2PB, UK.
ISBN 978-1-78646-857-4

www.packtpub.com

# Credits

**Author**
Giancarlo Zaccone

**Reviewer**
Jayani Withanawasam

**Commissioning Editor**
Veena Pagare

**Acquisition Editor**
Vinay Argekar

**Content Development Editor**
Sumeet Sawant

**Technical Editor**
Deepti Tuscano

**Copy Editor**
Alpha Singh

**Project Coordinator**
Shweta H Birwatkar

**Proofreader**
Safis Editing

**Indexer**
Mariammal Chettiyar

**Production Coordinator**
Nilesh Mohite

**Cover Work**
Nilesh Mohite

# About the Author

**Giancarlo Zaccone** has more than 10 years of experience managing research projects in both the scientific and industrial domains. He worked as researcher at the C.N.R, the National Research Council, where he was involved in projects related to parallel numerical computing and scientific visualization.

Currently, he is a senior software engineer at a consulting company developing and maintaining software systems for space and defence applications.

Giancarlo holds a master's degree in physics from the Federico II of Naples and a 2nd level postgraduate master course in scientific computing from La Sapienza of Rome.

He has already been a Packt author for the following book: *Python Parallel Programming Cookbook*.

You can contact him at https://it.linkedin.com/in/giancarlozaccone

# About the Reviewer

**Jayani Withanawasam** is a senior software engineer at Zaizi Asia - Research and Development team. She is the author of the book *Apache Mahout Essentials*, on scalable machine learning. She was a summit speaker at Alfresco Summit 2014 - London. Her talk was about applications of machine learning techniques in smart enterprise content management (ECM) solutions. She presented her research "Content Extraction and Context Inference based Information Retrieval" at the Women in Machine Learning (WiML) 2015 workshop, which was co-located with the Neural Information Processing Systems (NIPS) 2015 conference - Montreal, Canada.

Jayani is currently pursuing an MSc in Artificial Intelligence at the University of Moratuwa, Sri Lanka. She has strong research interests in machine learning and computer vision.

You can contact her at `https://lk.linkedin.com/in/jayaniwithanawasam`

# www.PacktPub.com

## eBooks, discount offers, and more

Did you know that Packt offers eBook versions of every book published, with PDF and ePub files available? You can upgrade to the eBook version at www.PacktPub.com and as a print book customer, you are entitled to a discount on the eBook copy. Get in touch with us at customercare@packtpub.com for more details.

At www.PacktPub.com, you can also read a collection of free technical articles, sign up for a range of free newsletters and receive exclusive discounts and offers on Packt books and eBooks.

https://www2.packtpub.com/books/subscription/packtlib

Do you need instant solutions to your IT questions? PacktLib is Packt's online digital book library. Here, you can search, access, and read Packt's entire library of books.

## Why subscribe?

- Fully searchable across every book published by Packt
- Copy and paste, print, and bookmark content
- On demand and accessible via a web browser

# Table of Contents

# Preface

TensorFlow is an open source software library used to implement machine learning and deep learning systems.

Behind these two names are hidden a series of powerful algorithms that share a common challenge: to allow a computer to learn how to automatically recognize complex patterns and make the smartest decisions possible.

Machine learning algorithms are supervised or unsupervised; simplifying as much as possible, we can say that the biggest difference is that in supervised learning the programmer instructs the computer how to do something, whereas in unsupervised learning the computer will learn all by itself.

Deep learning is instead a new area of machine learning research that has been introduced with the objective of moving machine learning closer to artificial intelligence goals. This means that deep learning algorithms try to operate like the human brain.

With the aim of conducting research in these fascinating areas, the Google team developed TensorFlow, which is the subject of this book.

To introduce TensorFlow's programming features, we have used the Python programming language. Python is fun and easy to use; it is a true general-purpose language and is quickly becoming a must-have tool in the arsenal of any self-respecting programmer.

It is not the aim of this book to completely describe all TensorFlow objects and methods; instead we will introduce the important system concepts and lead you up the learning curve as fast and efficiently as we can. Each chapter of the book presents a different aspect of TensorFlow, accompanied by several programming examples that reflect typical issues of machine and deep learning.

Although it is large and complex, TensorFlow is designed to be easy to use once you learn about its basic design and programming methodology.

The purpose of *Getting Started with TensorFlow* is to help you do just that.

Enjoy reading!

# What this book covers

*Chapter 1, TensorFlow – Basic Concepts,* contains general information on the structure of TensorFlow and the issues for which it was developed. It also provides the basic programming guidelines for the Python language and a first TensorFlow working session after the installation procedure. The chapter ends with a description of TensorBoard, a powerful tool for optimization and debugging.

*Chapter 2, Doing Math with TensorFlow,* describes the ability of mathematical processing of TensorFlow. It covers programming examples on basic algebra up to partial differential equations. Also, the basic data structure in TensorFlow, the tensor, is explained.

*Chapter 3, Starting with Machine Learning,* introduces some machine learning models. We start to implement the linear regression algorithm, which is concerned with modeling relationships between data. The main focus of the chapter is on solving two basic problems in machine learning; classification, that is, how to assign each new input to one of the possible given categories; and data clustering, which is the task of grouping a set of objects in such a way that objects in the same group are more similar to each other than to those in other groups.

*Chapter 4, Introducing Neural Networks,* provides a quick and detailed introduction of neural networks. These are mathematical models that represent the interconnection between elements, the artificial neurons. They are mathematical constructs that to some extent mimic the properties of living neurons. Neural networks build the foundation on which rests the architecture of deep learning algorithms. Two basic types of neural nets are then implemented: the Single Layer Perceptron and the Multi Layer Perceptron for classification problems.

*Chapter 5, Deep Learning,* gives an overview of deep learning algorithms. Only in recent years has deep learning collected a large number of results considered unthinkable a few years ago. We'll show how to implement two fundamental deep learning architectures, convolutional neural networks (CNN) and recurrent neural networks (RNN), for image recognition and speech translation problems respectively.

*Chapter 6, GPU Programming and Serving with TensorFlow,* shows the TensorFlow facilities for *GPU* computing and introduces *TensorFlow Serving,* a high-performance open source serving system for machine learning models designed for production environments and optimized for TensorFlow.

# What you need for this book

All the examples have been implemented using Python version 2.7 on an Ubuntu Linux 64-bit machine, including the TensorFlow library version 0.7.1.

You will also need the following Python modules (preferably the latest version):

- Pip
- Bazel
- Matplotlib
- NumPy
- Pandas

# Who this book is for

The reader should have a basic knowledge of programming and math concepts, and at the same time, want to be introduced to the topics of machine and deep learning. After reading this book, you will be able to master TensorFlow's features to build powerful applications.

# Conventions

In this book, you will find a number of text styles that distinguish between different kinds of information. Here are some examples of these styles and an explanation of their meaning.

Code words in text, database table names, folder names, filenames, file extensions, path names, dummy URLs, user input, and Twitter handles are shown as follows: "The instructions for flow control are `if`, `for`, and `while`."

Any command-line input or output is written as follows:

```
>>> myvar = 3
>>> myvar += 2
>>> myvar
5
>>> myvar -= 1
>>> myvar
4
```

**New terms** and **important words** are shown in bold. Words that you see on the screen, for example, in menus or dialog boxes, appear in the text like this: "The shortcuts in this book are based on the `Mac OS X 10.5+` scheme."

 Warnings or important notes appear in a box like this.

 Tips and tricks appear like this.

# Reader feedback

Feedback from our readers is always welcome. Let us know what you think about this book-what you liked or disliked. Reader feedback is important for us as it helps us develop titles that you will really get the most out of. To send us general feedback, simply e-mail `feedback@packtpub.com`, and mention the book's title in the subject of your message. If there is a topic that you have expertise in and you are interested in either writing or contributing to a book, see our author guide at `www.packtpub.com/authors`.

# Customer support

Now that you are the proud owner of a Packt book, we have a number of things to help you to get the most from your purchase.

# Downloading the example code

You can download the example code files for this book from your account at `http://www.packtpub.com`. If you purchased this book elsewhere, you can visit `http://www.packtpub.com/support` and register to have the files e-mailed directly to you.

You can download the code files by following these steps:

1. Log in or register to our website using your e-mail address and password.
2. Hover the mouse pointer on the **SUPPORT** tab at the top.
3. Click on **Code Downloads & Errata**.
4. Enter the name of the book in the **Search** box.
5. Select the book for which you're looking to download the code files.
6. Choose from the drop-down menu where you purchased this book from.
7. Click on **Code Download**.

Once the file is downloaded, please make sure that you unzip or extract the folder using the latest version of:

- WinRAR / 7-Zip for Windows
- Zipeg / iZip / UnRarX for Mac
- 7-Zip / PeaZip for Linux

The code bundle for the book is also hosted on GitHub at `https://github.com/PacktPublishing/Getting-Started-with-TensorFlow`. We also have other code bundles from our rich catalog of books and videos available at `https://github.com/PacktPublishing/`. Check them out!

# Downloading the color images of this book

We also provide you with a PDF file that has color images of the screenshots/diagrams used in this book. The color images will help you better understand the changes in the output. You can download this file from `http://www.packtpub.com/sites/default/files/downloads/GettingStartedwithTensorFlow_ColorImages.pdf`.

# Errata

Although we have taken every care to ensure the accuracy of our content, mistakes do happen. If you find a mistake in one of our books-maybe a mistake in the text or the code-we would be grateful if you could report this to us. By doing so, you can save other readers from frustration and help us improve subsequent versions of this book. If you find any errata, please report them by visiting `http://www.packtpub.com/submit-errata`, selecting your book, clicking on the **Errata Submission Form** link, and entering the details of your errata. Once your errata are verified, your submission will be accepted and the errata will be uploaded to our website or added to any list of existing errata under the Errata section of that title.

To view the previously submitted errata, go to https://www.packtpub.com/books/content/support and enter the name of the book in the search field. The required information will appear under the **Errata** section.

# Piracy

Piracy of copyrighted material on the Internet is an ongoing problem across all media. At Packt, we take the protection of our copyright and licenses very seriously. If you come across any illegal copies of our works in any form on the Internet, please provide us with the location address or website name immediately so that we can pursue a remedy.

Please contact us at copyright@packtpub.com with a link to the suspected pirated material.

We appreciate your help in protecting our authors and our ability to bring you valuable content.

# Questions

If you have a problem with any aspect of this book, you can contact us at questions@packtpub.com, and we will do our best to address the problem.

# 1
# TensorFlow – Basic Concepts

In this chapter, we'll cover the following topics:

- Machine learning and deep learning basics
- TensorFlow – A general overview
- Python basics
- Installing TensorFlow
- First working session
- Data Flow Graph
- TensorFlow programming model
- How to use TensorBoard

## Machine learning and deep learning basics

Machine learning is a branch of artificial intelligence, and more specifically of computer science, which deals with the study of systems and algorithms that can learn from data, synthesizing new knowledge from them.

The word learn intuitively suggests that a system based on machine learning, may, on the basis of the observation of previously processed data, *improve* its knowledge in order to achieve *better results in the future*, or provide *output closer* to the desired output for that particular system.

The ability of a program or a system based on machine learning to improve its performance in a particular task, thanks to *past experience*, is strongly linked to its ability *to recognize patterns in the data*. This theme, called *pattern recognition*, is therefore of vital importance and of increasing interest in the context of artificial intelligence; it is the basis of all machine learning techniques.

The training of a machine learning system can be done in different ways:

- Supervised learning
- Unsupervised learning

# Supervised learning

Supervised learning is the most common form of machine learning. With supervised learning, a set of examples, the training set, is submitted as input to the system during the *training phase*, where each example is *labeled* with the respective *desired output value*. For example, let's consider a **classification problem**, where the system must attribute some experimental observations in one of the N different classes already known. In this problem, the training set is presented as a sequence of pairs of the type { (X1, Y1), ....., (Xn, Yn) } where Xi are the input vectors (*feature vectors*) and Yi represents the desired class for the corresponding input vector. Most supervised learning algorithms share one characteristic: the training is performed by the minimization of a particular loss function (*cost function*), which represents the *output error* with respect to the desired output system.

The cost function most used for this type of training calculates the *standard deviation* between the desired output and the one supplied by the system. After training, the *accuracy* of the model is measured on a set of disjointed examples from the training set, the so-called *validation set*.

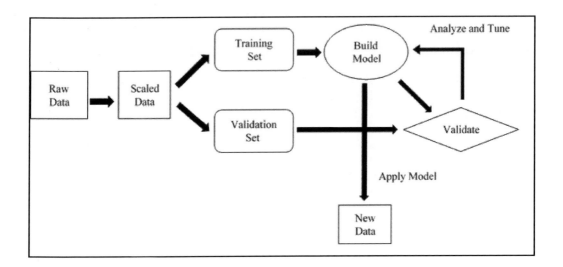

Supervised learning workflow

In this phase the *model's generalization capability* is then verified: we will test *if the output is correct* for an unused input during the training phase.

# Unsupervised learning

In unsupervised learning, the training examples provided by the system *are not labeled* with the related belonging class. The system, therefore, develops and organizes the data, looking for *common characteristics* among them, and changing them based on their internal knowledge.

Unsupervised learning algorithms are particularly used in *clustering problems*, in which a number of input examples are present, you do not know the class a priori, and you do not even know what the possible classes are, or how numerous they are. This is a clear case when you cannot use supervised learning, because you do not know a priori the number of classes.

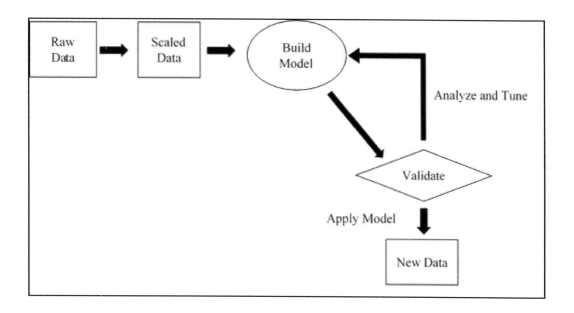

Unsupervised learning workflow

# Deep learning

Deep learning techniques represent a remarkable step forward taken by machine learning in recent decades, having provided results never seen before in many applications, such as image and speech recognition or **Natural Language Processing (NLP)**. There are several reasons that led to deep learning being developed and placed at the center of the field of machine learning only in recent decades. One reason, perhaps the main one, is surely represented by progress in hardware, with the availability of new processors, such as **graphics processing units (GPUs)**, which have greatly reduced the time needed for training networks, lowering them by a factor of 10 or 20. Another reason is certainly the ever more numerous datasets on which to train a system, needed to train architectures of a certain depth and with a high dimensionality for the input data.

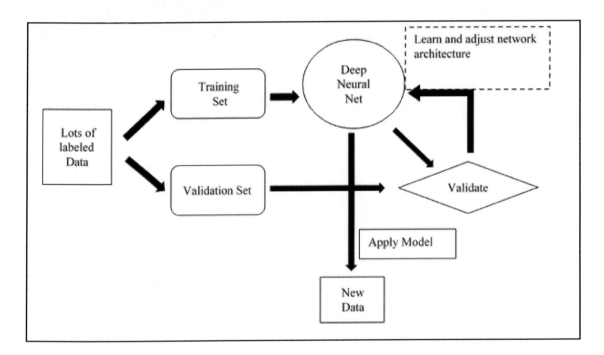

Deep learning workflow

Deep learning is based on the way the *human brain* processes information and learns, responding to external stimuli. It consists in a machine learning model at *several levels of representation* in which the deeper levels take as input the outputs of the previous levels, transforming them and always abstracting more. Each level corresponds in this hypothetical model to a different area of the cerebral cortex: when the brain receives images, it processes them through various stages such as *edge detection* and *form perception*, that is, from a *primitive* representation level to the *most complex*. For example, in an image classification problem, each block gradually extracts the *features*, at various levels of abstraction, inputting of data already processed, by means of *filtering operations*.

# TensorFlow – A general overview

TensorFlow (`https://www.tensorflow.org/`) is a software library, developed by Google Brain Team within Google's Machine Learning Intelligence research organization, for the purposes of conducting machine learning and deep neural network research. TensorFlow then combines the computational algebra of compilation optimization techniques, making easy the calculation of many mathematical expressions where the problem is the time required to perform the computation.

The main features include:

- Defining, optimizing, and efficiently calculating mathematical expressions involving multi-dimensional arrays (tensors).
- Programming support of deep neural networks and machine learning techniques.
- Transparent use of GPU computing, automating management and optimization of the same memory and the data used. You can write the same code and run it either on CPUs or GPUs. More specifically, TensorFlow will figure out which parts of the computation should be moved to the GPU.
- High scalability of computation across machines and huge data sets.

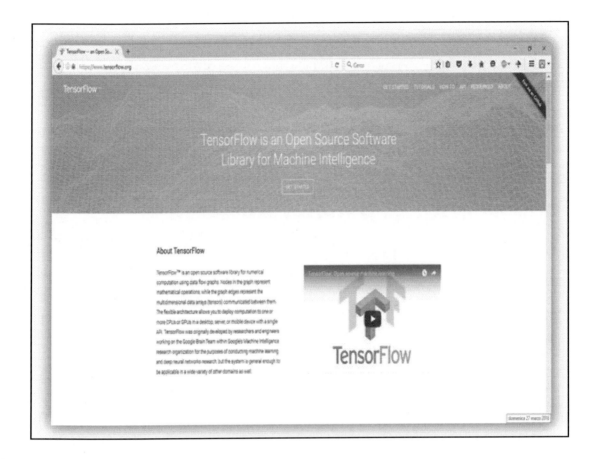

TensorFlow home page

TensorFlow is available with Python and C++ support, and we shall use Python 2.7 for learning, as indeed Python API is better supported and much easier to learn. The Python installation depends on your systems; the download page (https://www.python.org/downloads/) contains all the information needed for its installation. In the next section, we explain very briefly the main features of the Python language, with some programming examples.

# Python basics

Python is a strongly typed and dynamic language (data types are necessary but it is not necessary to explicitly declare them), case-sensitive (var and VAR are two different variables), and object-oriented (everything in Python is an object).

# Syntax

In Python, a line terminator is not required, and the blocks are specified with the indentation. Indent to begin a block and remove indentation to conclude it, that's all. Instructions that require an indented block end with a colon (:). Comments begin with the hash sign (#) and are single-line. Strings on multiple lines are used for multi-line comments. Assignments are accomplished with the equal sign (=). For equality tests we use the double equal (==) symbol. You can increase and decrease a value by using += and -= followed by the addend. This works with many data types, including strings. You can assign and use multiple variables on the same line.

Following are some examples:

```
>>> myvar = 3
>>> myvar += 2
>>> myvar
5
>>> myvar -= 1
>>> myvar
4
"""This is a comment"""
>>> mystring = "Hello"
>>> mystring += " world."
>>> print mystring
Hello world.
```

The following code swaps two variables in one line:

```
>>> myvar, mystring = mystring, myvar
```

# Data types

The most significant structures in Python are lists, tuples, and dictionaries. The sets are integrated in Python since version 2.5 (for previous versions, they are available in the sets library). Lists are similar to single-dimensional arrays but you can create lists that contain other lists. Dictionaries are arrays that contain pairs of keys and values (hash table), and tuples are immutable mono-dimensional objects. In Python arrays can be of any type, so you can mix integers, strings, and so on in your lists/dictionaries and tuples. The index of the first object in any type of array is always zero. Negative indices are allowed and counting from the end of the array, $-1$ is the last element. Variables can refer to functions.

```
>>> example = [1, ["list1", "list2"], ("one", "tuple")]
>>> mylist = ["Element 1", 2, 3.14]
>>> mylist [0]
"Element 1"
>>> mylist [-1]
3.14
>>> mydict = {"Key 1": "Val 1", 2: 3, "pi": 3.14}
>>> mydict ["pi"]
3.14
>>> mytuple = (1, 2, 3)
>>> myfunc = len
>>> print myfunc (mylist)
3
```

You can get an array range using a colon (:). Not specifying the starting index of the range implies the first element; not indicating the final index implies the last element. Negative indices count from the last element ($-1$ is the last element). Then run the following command:

```
>>> mylist = ["first element", 2, 3.14]
>>> print mylist [:]
['first element', 2, 3.1400000000000001]
>>> print mylist [0:2]
['first element', 2]
>>> print mylist [-3:-1]
['first element', 2]
>>> print mylist [1:]
[2, 3.14]
```

# Strings

Pythonstrings are indicated either with a single quotation mark (') or double (") and are allowed to use a notation within a delimited string on the other ("He said' hello '."It is valid). Strings of multiple lines are enclosed in triple (or single) quotes ("""). Python supports unicode; just use the syntax: "This is a unicode string". To insert values into a string , use the % operator (modulo) and a tuple. Each % is replaced by a tuple element, from left to right, and is permitted to use a dictionary for the replacements.

```
>>> print "Nome: %s\nNumber: %s\nString: %s" % (myclass.nome, 3, 3 * "-")
    Name: Poromenos
    Number: 3
    String: ---
    strString = """this is a string
    on multiple lines."""
>>> print "This %(verbo)s un %(name)s." % {"name": "test", "verb": "is"}
    This is a test.
```

# Control flow

The instructions for flow control are if, for, and while. There is the select control flow; in its place, we use if. The for control flow is used to enumerate the members of a list. To get a list of numbers, you use range (number).

```
rangelist = range(10)
>>> print rangelist
[0, 1, 2, 3, 4, 5, 6, 7, 8, 9]
```

Let's check if number is one of the numbers in the tuple:

```
for number in rangelist:
    if number in (3, 4, 7, 9):
        # "Break" ends the for instruction without the else clause
        break
    else:
        # "Continue" continues with the next iteration of the loop
        continue
else:
    # this is an optional "else"
    # executed only if the loop is not interrupted with "break".
    pass # it does nothing
if rangelist[1] == 2:
    print "the second element (lists are 0-based) is 2"
elif rangelist[1] == 3:
    print "the second element is 3"
```

```
else:
    print "I don't know"
while rangelist[1] == 1:
    pass
```

# Functions

Functions are declared with the keyword `def`. Any optional arguments must be declared after those that are mandatory and must have a value assigned. When calling functions using arguments to name you must also pass the value. Functions can return a tuple (tuple unpacking enables the return of multiple values). Lambda functions are in-line. Parameters are passed by reference, but immutable types (tuples, integers, strings, and so on) cannot be changed in the function. This happens because it is only passed through the position of the element in memory, and assigning another object to the variable results in the loss of the object reference earlier.

For example:

```
# equal to a def f(x): return x + 1
funzionevar = lambda x: x + 1
>>> print funzionevar(1)
2
def passing_example(my_list,my_int):
    my_list.append("new element")
    my_int = 4
    return my_list, my_int
>>> input_my_list = [1, 2, 3]
>>> input_my_int = 10
>>> print passing_example(input_my_list, input_my_int)
([1, 2, 3, 'new element'], 10)
>>> my_list
[1, 2, 3, 'new element']
>>> my_int
10
```

# Classes

Python supports multiple inheritance of classes. The variables and private methods are declared by convection (it is not a rule of language) by preceding them with two underscores (__). We can assign attributes (properties) to arbitrary instances of a class.

The following is an example:

```
class Myclass:
    common = 10
    def __init__(self):
        self.myvariable= 3
    def myfunc(self, arg1, arg2):
        return self.myvariable
# We create an instance of the class
>>> instance= Myclass()
>>> instance.myfunc(1, 2)
3
# This variable is shared by all instances
>>> instance2= Myclass()
>>> instance.common
10
>>> instance2.common
10
# Note here how we use the class name
# Instead of the instance.
>>> Myclass.common = 30
>>> instance.common
30
>>> instance2.common
30
# This does not update the variable in the class,
# Instead assign a new object to the variable
# of the first instance.
>>> instance.common = 10
>>> instance.common
10
>>> instance2.common
30
>>> Myclass.common = 50
# The value is not changed because "common" is an instance variable.
>>> instance.common
10
>>> instance2.common
50
# This class inherits from Myclass. Multiple inheritance
# is declared like this:
```

```
# class AltraClasse(Myclass1, Myclass2, MyclassN)
class AnotherClass(Myclass):
    # The topic "self" is automatically passed
    # and makes reference to instance of the class, so you can set
    # of instance variables as above, but within the class.
def __init__(self, arg1):
        self.myvariable= 3
        print arg1
>>> instance= AnotherClass ("hello")
hello
>>> instance.myfunc(1, 2)
3
# This class does not have a member (property) .test member, but
# We can add one all instance when we want. Note
# .test That will be a member of only one instance.
>>> instance.test = 10
>>> instance.test
10
```

# Exceptions

Exceptions in Python are handled with `try-except` blocks [exception_name]:

```
def my_func():
    try:
        # Division by zero causes an exception
        10 / 0
    except ZeroDivisionError:
        print "Oops, error"
    else:
        # no exception, let's proceed
        pass
    finally:
# This code is executed when the block
    # Try..except is already executed and all exceptions
    # Were handled, even if there is a new
    # Exception directly in the block.
        print "finish"
>>> my_func()
Oops, error.
finish
```

# Importing a library

External libraries are imported with `import [library name]`. You can also use the form `[libraryname] import [funcname]` to import individual features. Here's an example:

```
import random
from time import clock
randomint = random.randint(1, 100)
>>> print randomint
64
```

# Installing TensorFlow

The TensorFlow Python API supports Python 2.7 and Python 3.3+. The GPU version (Linux only) requires the Cuda Toolkit >= 7.0 and cuDNN >= v2.

When working in a Python environment, it is recommended you use `virtualenv`. It will isolate your Python configuration for different projects; using `virtualenv` will not overwrite existing versions of Python packages required by TensorFlow.

## Installing on Mac or Linux distributions

The following are the steps to installTensorFlow on Mac and Linux system:

1. First install pip and virtualenv (optional) if they are not already installed:

   For Ubuntu/Linux 64-bit:

   ```
   $ sudo apt-get install python-pip python-dev python-virtualenv
   ```

   For Mac OS X:

   ```
   $ sudo easy_install pip
   $ sudo pip install --upgrade virtualenv
   ```

2. Then you can create a virtual environment virtualenv. The following commands create a virtual environment virtualenv in the `~ / tensorflow` directory:

   ```
   $ virtualenv --system-site-packages ~/tensorflow
   ```

3. The next step is to activate virtualenv as follows:

```
$ source ~/tensorflow/bin/activate.csh
(tensorflow)$
```

4. Henceforth, the name of the environment we're working in precedes the command line. Once activated, Pip is used to installTensorFlow within it.

For Ubuntu/Linux 64-bit, CPU:

```
(tensorflow)$ pip install --upgrade
https://storage.googleapis.com/tensorflow/linux/cpu/tensorflow-0.5.0-cp27-n
one-linux_x86_64.whl
```

For Mac OS X, CPU:

```
(tensorflow)$ pip install --upgrade
https://storage.googleapis.com/tensorflow/mac/tensorflow-0.5.0-py2-none-any
.whl
```

If you want to use your GPU card with TensorFlow, then install another package. I recommend you visit the official documentation to see if your GPU meets the specifications required to support TensorFlow.

To enable your GPU with TensorFlow, you can refer to (`https://www.tensorflow.org/versions/r0.9/get_started/os_s etup.html#optional-linux-enable-gpu-support`) for a complete description.

Finally, when you've finished, you must disable the virtual environment:

```
(tensorflow)$ deactivate
```

Given the introductory nature of this book, I suggest the reader to visit the download and setup TensorFlow page at (`https://www.tensorflow.or g/versions/r0.7/get_started/os_setup.html#download-and-se tup`) to find more information about other ways to install TensorFlow.

# Installing on Windows

If you can't get a Linux-based system, you can install Ubuntu on a virtual machine; just use a free application called VirtualBox, which lets you create a virtual PC on Windows and install Ubuntu in the latter. So you can try the operating system without creating partitions or dealing with cumbersome procedures.

 After installing VirtualBox, you can install Ubuntu (www.ubuntu.com) and then follow the installation for Linux machines to install TensorFlow.

# Installation from source

However, it may happen that the Pip installation causes problems, particularly when using the visualization tool TensorBoard (see https://github.com/tensorflow/tensorflow/issues/530). To fix this problem, I suggest you build and install TensorFlow, starting form source files, through the following steps:

1. Clone the TensorFlow repository:

   ```
   git clone --recurse-submodules
   https://github.com/tensorflow/tensorflow
   ```

2. Install Bazel (dependencies and installer), following the instructions at:

   ```
   http://bazel.io/docs/install.html.
   ```

3. Run the Bazel installer:

   ```
   chmod +x bazel-version-installer-os.sh
   ./bazel-version-installer-os.sh --user
   ```

4. Install the Python dependencies:

   ```
   sudo apt-get install python-numpy swig python-dev
   ```

5. Configure (GPU or no GPU ?) your installation in the TensorFlow downloaded repository:

   ```
   ./configure
   ```

6. Create your own TensorFlow Pip package using `bazel`:

```
bazel build -c opt //tensorflow/tools/pip_package:build_pip_package
```

7. To build with GPU support, use `bazel build -c opt --config=cuda` followed again by:

```
//tensorflow/tools/pip_package:build_pip_package
```

8. Finally, install TensorBoard where the name of the `.whl` file will depend on your platform.

```
pip install /tmp/tensorflow_pkg/tensorflow-0.7.1-py2-none-
linux_x86_64.whl
```

9. Good Luck!

 Please refer to `https://www.tensorflow.org/versions/r0.7/get_started/os_s etup.html#installation-for-linux` for further information.

# Testing your TensorFlow installation

Open a terminal and type the following lines of code:

```
>>> import tensorflow as tf
>>> hello = tf.constant("hello TensorFlow!")
>>> sess=tf.Session()
```

To verify your installation, just type:

```
>>> print(sess.run(hello))
```

You should have the following output:

```
Hello TensorFlow!
>>>
```

# First working session

Finally it is time to move from theory to practice. I will use the Python 2.7 IDE to write all the examples. To get an initial idea of how to use TensorFlow, open the Python editor and write the following lines of code:

```
x = 1
y = x + 9
print(y)
import tensorflow as tf
x = tf.constant(1,name='x')
y = tf.Variable(x+9,name='y')
print(y)
```

As you can easily understand in the first three lines, the constant x, set equal to 1, is then added to 9 to set the new value of the variable y, and then the end result of the variable y is printed on the screen.

In the last four lines, we have translated according to TensorFlow library the first three variables.

If we run the program, we have the following output:

```
10
<tensorflow.python.ops.variables.Variable object at    0x7f30ccbf9190>
```

The TensorFlow translation of the first three lines of the program example produces a different result. Let's analyze them:

1. The following statement should never be missed if you want to use the TensorFlow library. It tells us that we are importing the library and call it tf:

```
import tensorflow as tf
```

2. We create a constant value called x, with a value equal to one:

```
x = tf.constant(1,name='x')
```

3. Then we create a variable called y. This variable is defined with the simple equation $y=x+9$:

```
y = tf.Variable(x+9,name='y')
```

4. Finally, print out the result:

```
print(y)
```

So how do we explain the different result? The difference lies in the variable definition. In fact, the variable y doesn't represent the current value of x + 9, instead it means: *when the variable y is computed, take the value of the constant x and add 9 to it*. This is the reason why the value of y has never been carried out. In the next section, I'll try to fix it.

So we open the Python IDE and enter the following lines:

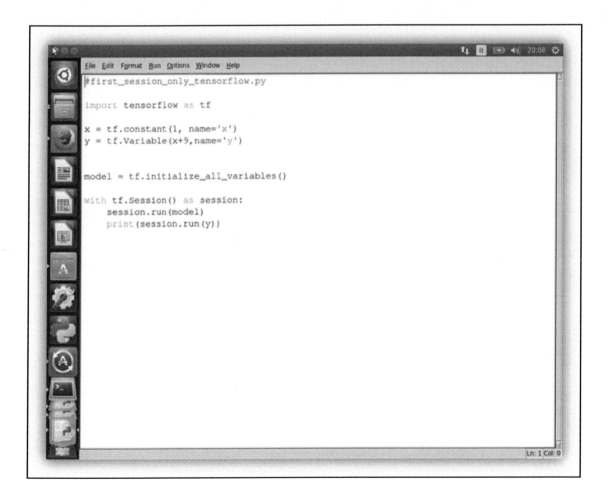

Running the preceding code, the output result is finally as follows:

```
10
```

We have removed the print instruction, but we have initialized the model variables:

```
model = tf.initialize_all_variables()
```

And, mostly, we have created a session for computing values. In the next step, we run the model, created previously, and finally run just the variable y and print out its current value.

```
with tf.Session() as session:
    session.run(model)
    print(session.run(y))
```

This is the magic trick that permits the correct result. In this fundamental step, the execution graph called Data Flow Graph is created in the session, with all the dependencies between the variables. The y variable depends on the variable x, and that value is transformed by adding 9 to it. The value is not computed until the session is executed.

This last example introduced another important feature in TensorFlow, the Data Flow Graph.

# Data Flow Graphs

A machine learning application is the result of the repeated computation of complex mathematical expressions. In TensorFlow, a computation is described using the Data Flow Graph, where each *node* in the graph represents the instance of a mathematical operation (multiply, add, divide, and so on), and each *edge* is a multi-dimensional data set (*tensors*) on which the operations are performed.

TensorFlow supports these constructs and these operators. Let's see in detail how nodes and edges are managed by TensorFlow:

- **Node**: In TensorFlow, each node represents the instantion of an operation. Each operation has >= inputs and >= 0 outputs.
- **Edges**: In TensorFlow, there are two types of edge:
    - **Normal Edges**: They are carriers of data structures (tensors), where an output of one operation (from one node) becomes the input for another operation.

- **Special Edges**: These edges are not data carriers between the output of a node (operator) and the input of another node. A special edge indicates a control dependency between two nodes. Let's suppose we have two nodes **A** and **B** and a special edges connecting **A** to **B**; it means that **B** will start its operation only when the operation in **A** ends. Special edges are used in Data Flow Graph to set the happens-before relationship between operations on the tensors.

Let's explore some features in Data Flow Graph in greater detail:

- **Operation**: This represents an abstract computation, such as adding or multiplying matrices. An operation manages tensors. It can just be polymorphic: the same operation can manipulate different tensor element types. For example, the addition of two int32 tensors, the addition of two float tensors, and so on.
- **Kernel**: This represents the concrete implementation of that operation. A kernel defines the implementation of the operation on a particular device. For example, an add matrix operation can have a CPU implementation and a GPU one. In the following section, we have introduced the concept of sessions to create a del execution graph in TensorFlow. Let's explain this topic:
- **Session**: When the client program has to establish communication with the TensorFlow runtime system, a session must be created. As soon as the session is created for a client, an initial graph is created and is empty. It has two fundamental methods:
    - `session.extend`: In a computation, the user can extend the execution graph, requesting to add more operations (nodes) and edges (data).
    - `session.run`: Using TensorFlow, sessions are created with some graphs, and these full graphs are executed to get some outputs, or sometimes, subgraphs are executed thousands/millions of times using run invocations. Basically, the method runs the execution graph to provide outputs.

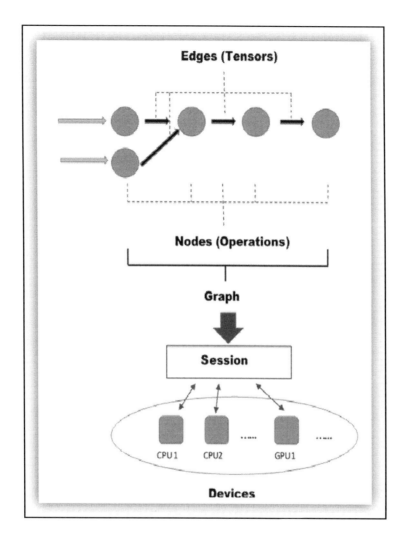

Features in Data Flow Graph

# TensorFlow programming model

Adopting Data Flow Graph as execution model, you divide the data flow design (graph building and data flow) from its execution (CPU, GPU cards, or a combination), using a single programming interface that hides all the complexities. It also defines what the programming model should be like in TensorFlow.

Let's consider the simple problem of multiplying two integers, namely a and b.

The following are the steps required for this simple problem:

1. Define and initialize the variables. Each variable should define the state of a current execution. After importing the TensorFlow module in Python:

```
import tensorflow as tf
```

2. We define the variables a and b involved in the computation. These are defined via a more basic structure, called the placeholder:

```
a = tf.placeholder("int32")
b = tf.placeholder("int32")
```

3. A placeholder allows us to create our operations and to build our computation graph, *without needing* the data.
4. Then we use these variables, as inputs for TensorFlow's function mul:

```
y = tf.mul(a,b)
this function will return the result of the multiplication the input
integers a and b.
```

5. Manage the execution flow, this means that we must build a *session*:

```
sess = tf.Session()
```

6. Visualize the results. We run our model on the variables a and b, feeding data into the data flow graph through the placeholders previously defined.

```
print sess.run(y , feed_dict={a: 2, b: 5})
```

# How to use TensorBoard

TensorBoard is a visualization tool, devoted to analyzing Data Flow Graph and also to better understand the machine learning models. It can view different types of statistics about the parameters and details of any part of a computer graph graphically. It often happens that a graph of computation can be very complex. A deep neural network can have up to 36,000 nodes. For this reason, TensorBoard collapses nodes in high-level blocks, highlighting the groups with identical structures. Doing so allows a better analysis of the graph, focusing only on the core sections of the computation graph. Also, the visualization process is interactive; user can pan, zoom, and expand the nodes to display the details.

The following figure shows a neural network model with TensorBoard:

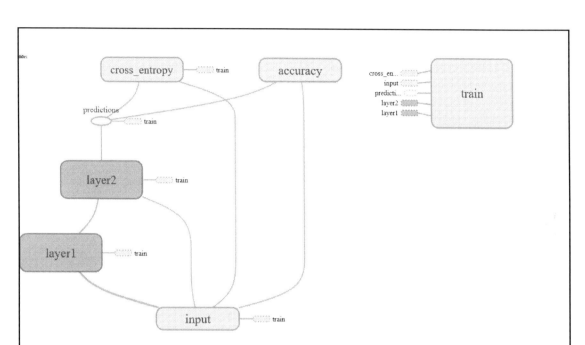

A TensorBoard visualization example

TensorBoard's algorithms collapse nodes into high-level blocks and highlight groups with the same structures, while also separating out high-degree nodes. The visualization tool is also interactive: the users can pan, zoom in, expand, and collapse the nodes.

TensorBoard is equally useful in the development and tuning of a machine learning model. For this reason, TensorFlow lets you insert so-called **summary operations** into the graph. These summary operations monitor changing values (during the execution of a computation) written in a log file. Then TensorBoard is configured to watch this log file with summary information and display how this information changes over time.

Let's consider a basic example to understand the usage of TensorBoard. We have the following example:

```
import tensorflow as tf
a = tf.constant(10,name="a")
b = tf.constant(90,name="b")
y = tf.Variable(a+b*2, name="y")
```

```
model = tf.initialize_all_variables()
with tf.Session() as session:
    merged = tf.merge_all_summaries()
    writer = tf.train.SummaryWriter\
                     ("/tmp/tensorflowlogs",session.graph)
     session.run(model)
    print(session.run(y))
```

That gives the following result:

```
190
```

Let's point into the session management. The first instruction to consider is as follows:

```
merged = tf.merge_all_summaries()
```

This instruction must merge all the summaries collected in the default graph.

Then we create `SummaryWriter`. It will write all the summaries (in this case the execution graph) obtained from the code's execution into the `/tmp/tensorflowlogs` directory:

```
writer = tf.train.SummaryWriter\
                 ("/tmp/tensorflowlogs",session.graph)
```

Finally, we run the model and so build the Data Flow Graph:

```
session.run(model)
print(session.run(y))
```

The use of TensorBoard is very simple. Let's open a terminal and enter the following:

```
$tensorboard --logdir=/tmp/tensorflowlogs
```

A message such as the following should appear:

```
startig tensorboard on port 6006
```

Then, by opening a web browser, we should display the Data Flow Graph with auxiliary nodes:

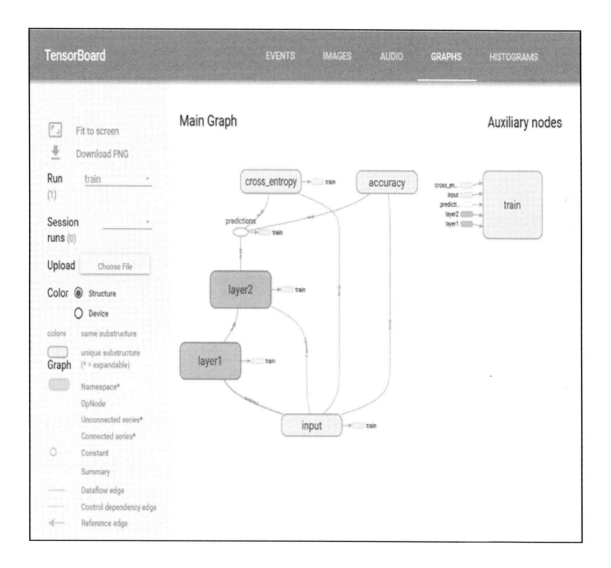

Data Flow Graph display with TensorBoard

Now we will be able to explore the Data Flow Graph:

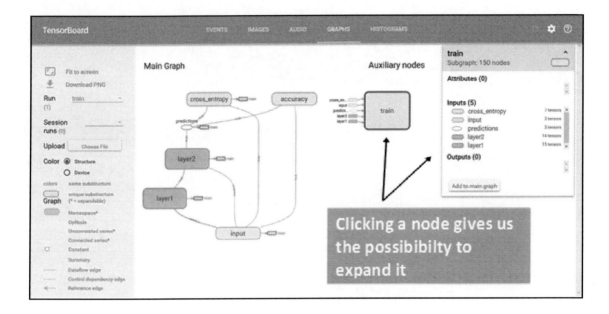

Explore the Data Flow Graph display with TensorBoard

TensorBoard uses special icons for constants and summary nodes. To summarize, we report in the next figure the table of node symbols displayed:

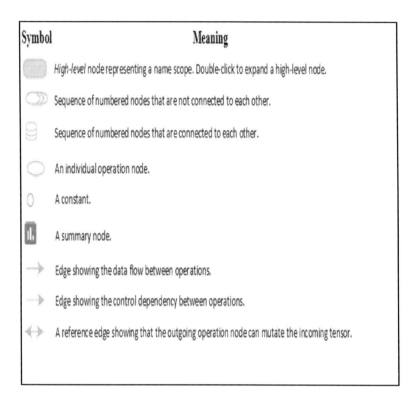

Node symbols in TensorBoard

# Summary

In this chapter, we introduced the main topics: **machine learning** and **deep learning**. While machine learning explores the study and construction of algorithms that can learn from, and make predictions on data, deep learning is based precisely on the way the *human brain processes information and learns*, responding to external stimuli.

In this vast scientific research and practical application area, we can firmly place the **TensorFlow** software library, developed by the Google's research group for artificial intelligence (Google Brain Project) and released as open source software on November 9, 2015.

After electing the **Python** programming language as the development tool for our examples and applications, we saw how to install and compile the library, and then carried out a first working session. This allowed us to introduce the execution model of TensorFlow and **Data Flow Graph**. It led us to define what our programming model should be.

The chapter ended with an example of how to use an important tool for debugging machine learning applications: **TensorBoard**.

In the next chapter, we will continue our journey into the TensorFlow library, with the intention of showing its versatility. Starting from the fundamental concept, tensors, we will see how to use the library for purely math applications.

# 2
# Doing Math with TensorFlow

In this chapter, we will cover the following topics:

- The tensor data structure
- Handling tensors with TensorFlow
- Complex numbers and fractals
- Computing derivatives
- Random numbers
- Solving partial differential equations

## The tensor data structure

Tensors are the basic data structures in TensorFlow. As we have already said, they represent the connecting edges in a Data Flow Graph. A tensor simply identifies a multidimensional array or list.

It can be identified by three parameters, `rank`, `shape`, and `type`:

- `rank`: Each tensor is described by a unit of dimensionality called rank. It identifies the number of dimensions of the tensor. For this reason, a rank is known as order or n-dimensions of a tensor (for example, a rank 2 tensor is a matrix and a rank 1 tensor is a vector).
- `shape`: The shape of a tensor is the number of rows and columns it has.
- `type`: It is the data type assigned to the tensor's elements.

Well, now we take confidence with this fundamental data structure. To build a tensor, we can:

- Build an n-dimensional array; for example, by using the NumPy library
- Convert the n-dimensional array into a TensorFlow tensor

Once we obtain the tensor, we can handle it using the TensorFlow operators. The following figure provides a visual explanation of the concepts introduced:

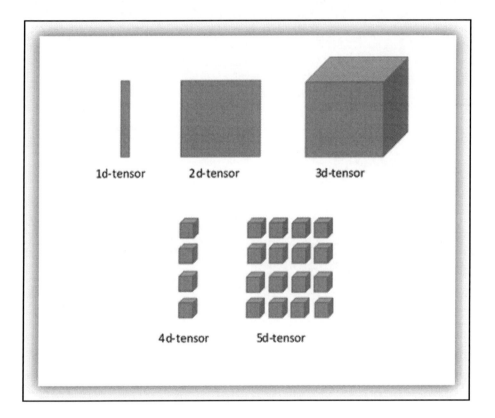

Visualization of multidimensional tensors

# One-dimensional tensors

To build a one-dimensional tensor, we use the Numpy array(s) command, where s is a Python list:

```
>>> import numpy as np
>>> tensor_1d = np.array([1.3, 1, 4.0, 23.99])
```

Unlike a Python list, the commas between the elements are not shown:

```
>>> print tensor_1d
[  1.3    1.     4.     23.99]
```

The indexing is the same as Python lists. The first element has position 0, the third element has position 2, and so on:

```
>>> print tensor_1d[0]
1.3
>>> print tensor_1d[2]
4.0
```

Finally, you can view the basic attributes of the tensor, the rank of the tensor:

```
>>> tensor_1d.ndim
1
```

The tuple of the tensor's dimension is as follows:

```
>>> tensor_1d.shape
(4L,)
```

The tensor's shape has just four values in a row.

The *data type* in the tensor:

```
>>> tensor_1d.dtype
dtype('float64')
```

Now, let's see how to convert a NumPy array into a TensorFlow tensor:

```
import TensorFlow as tf
```

The TensorFlow function `tf_convert_to_tensor` converts Python objects of various types to tensor objects. It accepts tensor objects, Numpy arrays, Python lists, and Python scalars:

```
tf_tensor=tf.convert_to_tensor(tensor_1d,dtype=tf.float64)
```

Running the `Session`, we can visualize the tensor and its elements as follows:

```
with tf.Session() as sess:
    print sess.run(tf_tensor)
    print sess.run(tf_tensor[0])
    print sess.run(tf_tensor[2])
```

That gives the following results:

```
>>
[  1.3    1.     4.     23.99]
1.3
4.0
>>>
```

# Two-dimensional tensors

To create a two-dimensional tensor or matrix, we again use array(s), but s will be a sequence of array:

```
>>> import numpy as np

>>> tensor_2d=np.array([(1,2,3,4),(4,5,6,7),(8,9,10,11),(12,13,14,15)])

>>> print tensor_2d
[[ 1  2  3  4]
 [ 4  5  6  7]
 [ 8  9 10 11]
 [12 13 14 15]]
>>>
```

A value in `tensor_2d` is identified by the expression `tensor_2d[row,col]`, where `row` is the row position and `col` is the column position:

```
>>> tensor_2d[3][3]
15
```

You can also use the slice operator : to extract a submatrix:

```
>>> tensor_2d[0:2,0:2]
array([[1, 2],
       [4, 5]])
```

In this case, we extracted a 2×2 submatrix, containing row 0 and 1, and columns 0 and 1 of `tensor_2d`. TensorFlow has its own slice operator. In the next subsection we will see how to use it.

# Tensor handling

Let's see how we can apply a little more complex operations to these data structures. Consider the following code:

1. Import the libraries:

```
import TensorFlow as tf
import numpy as np
```

2. Let's build two integer arrays. These represents two 3×3 matrices:

```
matrix1 = np.array([(2,2,2),(2,2,2),(2,2,2)],dtype='int32')
matrix2 = np.array([(1,1,1),(1,1,1),(1,1,1)],dtype='int32')
```

3. Visualize them:

```
print "matrix1  ="
print matrix1

print "matrix2 ="
print matrix2
```

4. To use these matrices in our TensorFlow environment, they must be transformed into a tensor data structure:

```
matrix1 = tf.constant(matrix1)
matrix2 = tf.constant(matrix2)
```

5. We used the TensorFlow `constant` operator to perform the transformation.

6.  The matrices are ready to be manipulated with TensorFlow operators. In this case, we calculate a matrix multiplication and a matrix sum:

```
matrix_product = tf.matmul(matrix1, matrix2)
matrix_sum = tf.add(matrix1,matrix2)
```

7.  The following matrix will be used to compute a matrix determinant:

```
matrix_3 = np.array([(2,7,2),(1,4,2),(9,0,2)],dtype='float32')

print "matrix3 ="
print matrix_3

matrix_det = tf.matrix_determinant(matrix_3)
```

8.  It's time to create our graph and run the session, with the tensors and operators created:

```
with tf.Session() as sess:
    result1 = sess.run(matrix_product)
    result2 = sess.run(matrix_sum)
    result3 = sess.run(matrix_det)
```

9.  The results will be printed out by running the following command:

```
print "matrix1*matrix2 ="
print result1

print "matrix1 + matrix2 ="
print result2

print "matrix3 determinant result ="
print result3
```

The following figure shows the results, after running the code:

TensorFlow provides numerous math operations on tensors. The following table summarizes them:

| TensorFlow operator | Description |
|---|---|
| tf.add | Returns the sum |
| tf.sub | Returns subtraction |
| tf.mul | Returns the multiplication |
| tf.div | Returns the division |

| `tf.mod` | Returns the module |
|---|---|
| `tf.abs` | Returns the absolute value |
| `tf.neg` | Returns the negative value |
| `tf.sign` | Returns the sign |
| `tf.inv` | Returns the inverse |
| `tf.square` | Returns the square |
| `tf.round` | Returns the nearest integer |
| `tf.sqrt` | Returns the square root |
| `tf.pow` | Returns the power |
| `tf.exp` | Returns the exponential |
| `tf.log` | Returns the logarithm |
| `tf.maximum` | Returns the maximum |
| `tf.minimum` | Returns the minimum |
| `tf.cos` | Returns the cosine |
| `tf.sin` | Returns the sine |

# Three-dimensional tensors

The following commands build a three-dimensional tensor:

```
>>> import numpy as np
>>> tensor_3d = np.array([[[1,2],[3,4]],[[5,6],[7,8]]])
>>> print tensor_3d
[[[1 2]
  [3 4]]

 [[5 6]
  [7 8]]]
>>>
```

The three-dimensional tensor created is a 2x2x2 matrix:

```
>>> tensor_3d.shape
(2L, 2L, 2L)
```

To retrieve an element from a three-dimensional tensor, we use an expression of the following form:

```
tensor_3d[plane,row,col]
```

Following these settings:

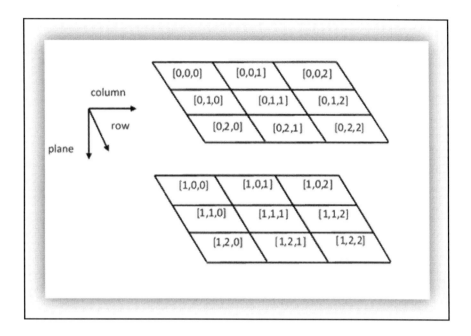

Matrix 3×3 representation

So all the four elements in the first plane identified by the value of the variable plane equal to zero:

```
>>> tensor_3d[0,0,0]
1
>>> tensor_3d[0,0,1]
2
>>> tensor_3d[0,1,0]
3
>>> tensor_3d[0,1,1]
4
```

The three-dimensional tensors allow to introduce the next topic, linked to the manipulation of images but more generally introduces us to operate as simple transformations on tensors.

# Handling tensors with TensorFlow

TensorFlow is designed to handle tensors of all sizes and operators that can be used to manipulate them. In this example, in order to see array manipulations, we are going to work with a digital image. As you probably know, a color digital image that is a MxNx3 size matrix (a three order tensor), whose components correspond to the components of red, green, and blue in the image (RGB space), means that each feature in the rectangular box for the RGB image will be specified by three coordinates, $i$, $j$, and $k$.

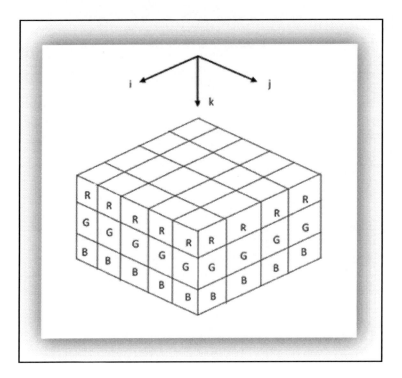

The RGB tensor

The first thing I want to show you is how to upload an image, and then to extract a sub-image from the original, using the TensorFlow slice operator.

# Prepare the input data

Using the `imread` command in matplotlib, we import a digital image in standard format colors (JPG, BMP, TIF):

```
import matplotlib.image as mp_image
filename = "packt.jpeg"
input_image = mp_image.imread(filename)
```

However, we can see the `rank` and the `shape` of the tensor:

```
print 'input dim = {}'.format(input_image.ndim)
print 'input shape = {}'.format(input_image.shape)
```

You'll see the output, which is (80, 144, 3). This means the image is 80 pixels high, 144 pixels wide, and 3 colors deep.

Finally, using `matplotlib`, it is possible to visualize the imported image:

```
import matplotlib.pyplot as plt
plt.imshow(input_image)
plt.show()
```

The starting image

In this example, slice is a bidimensional segment of the starting image, where each pixel has the RGB components, so we need a placeholder to store all the values of the slice:

```
import TensorFlow as tf
 my_image = tf.placeholder("uint8",[None,None,3])
```

For the last dimension, we'll need only three values. Then we use the TensorFlow operator slice to create a sub-image:

```
slice = tf.slice(my_image,[10,0,0],[16,-1,-1])
```

The last step is to build a TensorFlow working session:

```
with tf.Session() as session:
    result = session.run(slice,feed_dict={my_image: input_image})
    print(result.shape)

plt.imshow(result)
plt.show()
```

The resulting shape is then as the following image shows:

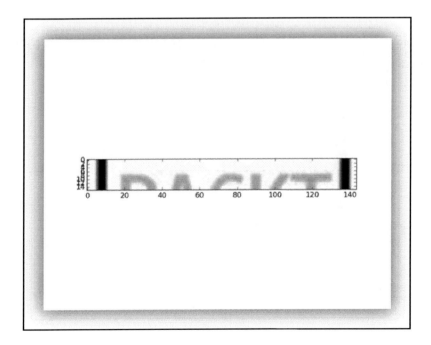

The input image after the slice

In this next example, we will perform a geometric transformation of the input image, using the transpose operator:

```
import TensorFlow as tf
```

We associate the input image to a variable we call x:

```
x = tf.Variable(input_image,name='x')
```

We then initialize our model:

```
model = tf.initialize_all_variables()
```

Next, we build up the session with that we run our code:

```
with tf.Session() as session:
```

To perform the transpose of our matrix, use the transpose function of TensorFlow. This method performs a swap between the axes 0 and 1 of the input matrix, while the z axis is left unchanged:

```
    x = tf.transpose(x, perm=[1,0,2])
    session.run(model)
    result=session.run(x)

plt.imshow(result)
plt.show()
```

The result is the following:

The transposed image

# Complex numbers and fractals

First of all, we look at how Python handles complex numbers. It is a simple matter. For example, setting x = 5 + 4j in Python, we must write the following:

```
>>> x = 5.+4j
```

It means that >>> x is equal to 5+4j.

At the same time, you can write the following:

```
>>> x = complex(5,4)
>>> x
(5+4j)
```

We also note that:

- Python uses `j` to mean $\sqrt{-1}$ instead of `i` in math.
- If you put a number before the `j`, Python will consider it as an imaginary number, otherwise, its a variable. It means that if you want to write the imaginary number `i`, you must write `1j` rather than `j`.

To get the real and imaginary parts of a Python complex number, you can use the following:

```
>>> x.real
5.0
>>> x.imag
4.0
>>>
```

We turn now to our problem, namely how to display the fractals with TensorFlow. The Mandelbrot set is one of the most famous fractals. A fractal is a geometric object that is repeated in its structure at different scales. Fractals are very common in nature, and an example is the coast of Great Britain.

The Mandelbrot set is defined for the complex numbers $c$ for which the following succession is true and bounded:

$$Z(n+1) = Z(n)^2 + c, \text{ where } Z(0) = 0$$

The set is named after its creator Benoît Mandelbrot, a Polish mathematician famous for making famous fractals. However, he was able to give a shape or graphic representation to the set of Mandelbrot only with the help of computer programming. In 1985, he published in Scientific American the first algorithm to calculate the Mandelbrot set. The algorithm (for each point complex point $Z$):

1. $Z$ has initial value equal to $0$, $Z(0) = 0$.
2. Choose the complex number $c$ as the current point. In the Cartesian plane, the abscissa axis (horizontal line) represents the real part, while the axis of ordinates (vertical line) represents the imaginary part of $c$.
3. Iteration: $Z(n + 1) = Z(n)^2 + c$
   - Stop when $Z(n)^2$ is larger than the maximum radius;

Now we see through simple steps how we can translate the algorithm mentioned earlier using TensorFlow.

# Prepare the data for Mandelbrot set

Import the necessary libraries to our example:

```
import TensorFlow as tf
import numpy as np
import matplotlib.pyplot as plt
```

We build a complex grid that will contain our Mandelbrot's set. The region of the complex plane is between $-1.3$ and $+1.3$ on the real axis and between $-2j$ and $+1j$ on the imaginary axis. Each pixel location in each image will represent a different complex value, $z$:

```
Y, X = np.mgrid[-1.3:1.3:0.005, -2:1:0.005]
Z = X+1j*Y
c = tf.constant(Z.astype(np.complex64))
```

Then we define data structures, or the tensor TensorFlow that contains all the data to be included in the calculation. We then define two variables. The first is the one on which we will make our iteration. It has the same dimensions as the complex grid, but it is declared as variable, that is, its values will change in the course of the calculation:

```
zs = tf.Variable(c)
```

The next variable is initialized to zero. It also has the same size as the variable $zs$:

```
ns = tf.Variable(tf.zeros_like(c, tf.float32))
```

# Build and execute the Data Flow Graph for Mandelbrot's set

Instead to introduce a session we instantiate an `InteractiveSession()`:

```
sess = tf.InteractiveSession()
```

It requires, as we shall see, the `Tensor.eval()` and `Operation.run()` methods. Then we initialize all the variables involved through the `run()` method:

```
tf.initialize_all_variables().run()
```

Start the iteration:

```
zs_ = zs*zs + c
```

Define the stop condition of the iteration:

```
not_diverged = tf.complex_abs(zs_) < 4
```

Then we use the group operator that groups multiple operations:

```
step = tf.group(zs.assign(zs_),\
          ns.assign_add(tf.cast(not_diverged, tf.float32)))
```

The first operation is the step iteration $Z(n+1) = Z(n)2 + c$ to create a new value.

The second operation adds this value to the correspondent element variable in `ns`. When this `op` finishes, all ops in input have finished. This operator has no output.

Then we run the operator for two hundred steps:

```
for i in range(200): step.run()
```

# Visualize the result for Mandelbrot's set

The result will be the tensor `ns.eval()`. Using matplotlib, let's visualize the result:

```
plt.imshow(ns.eval())
plt.show()
```

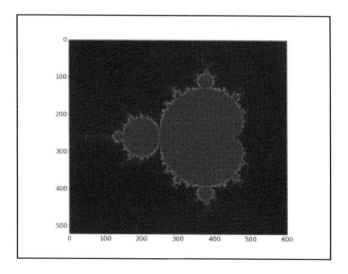

The Mandelbrot set

Of course, the Mandelbrot set is not the only fractal we can visualize. Julia sets are fractals that have been named after Gaston Maurice Julia for his work in this field. Their building process is very similar to that used for the Mandelbrot set.

# Prepare the data for Julia's set

Let's define the output complex plane. It is between $-2$ and $+2$ on the real axis and between $-2j$ and $+2j$ on the imaginary axis:

```
Y, X = np.mgrid[-2:2:0.005, -2:2:0.005]
```

And the current point location:

```
Z = X+1j*Y
```

The definition of the Julia's set requires redefing Z as a constant tensor:

```
Z = tf.constant(Z.astype("complex64"))
```

Thus the input tensors supporting our calculation is as follows:

```
zs = tf.Variable(Z)
ns = tf.Variable(tf.zeros_like(Z, "float32"))
```

# Build and execute the Data Flow Graph for Julia's set

As in the previous example, we create our own interactive session:

```
sess = tf.InteractiveSession()
```

We then initialize the input tensors:

```
tf.initialize_all_variables().run()
```

To compute the new values of the Julia set, we will use the iterative formula $Z(n+1) = Z(n)2 - c$, where the initial point $c$ will be equal to the imaginary number $0.75i$:

```
c = complex(0.0,0.75)
zs_ = zs*zs - c
```

The grouping operator and the stop iteration's condition will be the same as in the Mandelbrot computation:

```
not_diverged = tf.complex_abs(zs_) < 4

step = tf.group(zs.assign(zs_),\
                ns.assign_add(tf.cast(not_diverged, "float32")))
```

Finally, we run the operator for two hundred steps:

```
for i in range(200): step.run()
```

# Visualize the result

To visualize the result run the following command:

```
plt.imshow(ns.eval())
plt.show()
```

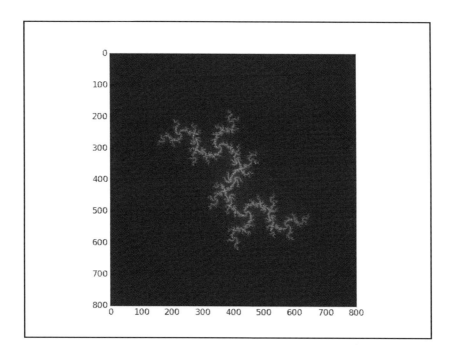

The Julia set

# Computing gradients

TensorFlow has functions to solve other more complex tasks. For example, we will use a mathematical operator that calculates the derivative of y with respect to its expression x parameter. For this purpose, we use the `tf.gradients()` function.

Let us consider the math function $y = 2x^2$. We want to compute the gradient di y with respect to x=1. The following is the code to compute this gradient:

1. First, import the TensorFlow library:

```
import TensorFlow as tf
```

2. The x variable is the independent variable of the function:

```
x = tf.placeholder(tf.float32)
```

3. Let's build the function:

```
y =  2*x*x
```

4. Finally, we call the `tf.gradients()` function with y and x as arguments:

```
var_grad = tf.gradients(y, x)
```

5. To evaluate the gradient, we must build a session:

```
with tf.Session() as session:
```

6. The gradient will be evaluated on the variable x=1:

```
var_grad_val = session.run(var_grad, feed_dict={x:1})
```

7. The `var_grad_val` value is the feed result, to be printed:

```
print(var_grad_val)
```

8. That gives the following result:

```
>>
[4.0]
>>
```

# Random numbers

The generation of random numbers is essential in machine learning and within the training algorithms. When random numbers are generated by a computer, they are generated by a **Pseudo Random Number Generator (PRNG)**. The term pseudo comes from the fact that the computer is a stain logically programmed running of instructions that can only simulate randomness. Despite this logical limitation, computers are very efficient at generating random numbers. TensorFlow provides operators to create random tensors with different distributions.

# Uniform distribution

Generally, when we need to work with random numbers, we try to get repeated values with the same frequency, uniformly distributed. The operator TensorFlow provides values between `minval` and `maxval`, all with the same probability. Let's see a simple example code:

```
random_uniform(shape, minval, maxval, dtype, seed, name)
```

We import the `TensorFlow` library and `matplotlib` to display the results:

```
import TensorFlow as tf
import matplotlib.pyplot as plt
```

The `uniform` variable is a 1-dimensional tensor, the elements `100`, containing values ranging from 0 to 1, distributed with the same probability:

```
uniform = tf.random_uniform([100],minval=0,maxval=1,dtype=tf.float32)
```

Let's define the session:

```
sess = tf.Session()
```

In our session, we evaluate the tensor uniform, using the `eval ()` operator:

```
with tf.Session() as session:
    print uniform.eval()
    plt.hist(uniform.eval(),normed=True)
    plt.show()
```

As you can see, all intermediate values between 0 and 1 have approximately the same frequency. This behavior is called uniform distribution. The result of execution is therefore as follows:

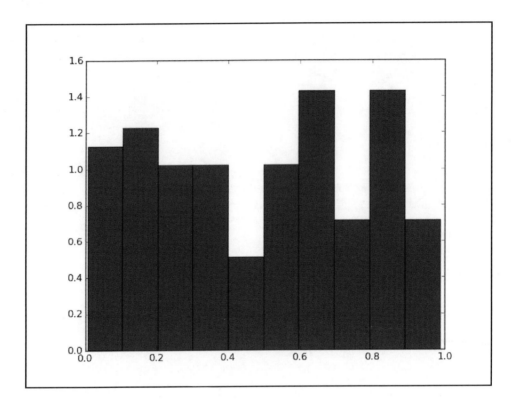

Uniform distribution

# Normal distribution

In some specific cases, you may need to generate random numbers that differ by a few units. In this case, we used the *normal distribution of random numbers*, also called *Gaussian distribution*, that increases the probability of the next issues extraction at 0. Each integer represents the standard deviation. As shown from the future issues to the margins of the range have a very low chance of being extracted. The following is the implementation with TensorFlow:

```
import TensorFlow as tf
import matplotlib.pyplot as plt
```

```
norm = tf.random_normal([100], mean=0, stddev=2)
with tf.Session() as session:
    plt.hist(norm.eval(),normed=True)
    plt.show()
```

We created a `1d-tensor` of shape `[100]` consisting of random normal values, with mean equal to 0 and standard deviation equal to 2, using the operator `tf.random_normal`. The following is the result:

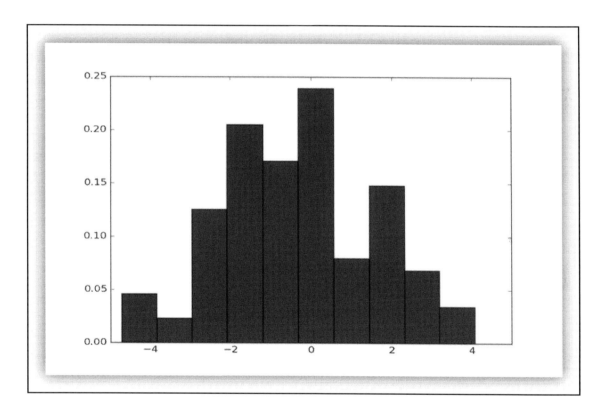

Normal distribution

# Generating random numbers with seeds

We recall that our sequence is *pseudo-random*, because the values are calculated using a deterministic algorithm and probability plays no real role. The seed is just a starting point for the sequence and if you start from the same seed you will end up with the same sequence. This is very useful, for example, to debug your code, when you are searching for an error in a program and you must be able to reproduce the problem because every run would be different.

Consider the following example where we have two uniform distributions:

```
uniform_with_seed = tf.random_uniform([1], seed=1)
uniform_without_seed = tf.random_uniform([1])
```

In the first uniform distribution, we began with the seed = 1. This means that repeatedly evaluating the two distributions, the first uniform distribution will always generate *the same sequence* of values:

```
print("First Run")
with tf.Session() as first_session:
print("uniform with (seed = 1) = {}"\
.format(first_session.run(uniform_with_seed)))
print("uniform with (seed = 1) = {}"\
.format(first_session.run(uniform_with_seed)))
print("uniform without seed = {}"\
.format(first_session.run(uniform_without_seed)))
print("uniform without seed = {}"\
.format(first_session.run(uniform_without_seed)))
print("Second Run")
with tf.Session() as second_session:
print("uniform with (seed = 1) = {}\
.format(second_session.run(uniform_with_seed)))
print("uniform with (seed = 1) = {}\
.format(second_session.run(uniform_with_seed)))
print("uniform without seed = {}"\
.format(second_session.run(uniform_without_seed)))
print("uniform without seed = {}"\
.format(second_session.run(uniform_without_seed)))
```

As you can see, this is the end result. The uniform distribution with `seed = 1` always gives the same result:

```
>>>
First Run
uniform with (seed = 1) = [ 0.23903739]
uniform with (seed = 1) = [ 0.22267115]
uniform without seed = [ 0.92157185]
uniform without seed = [ 0.43226039]
Second Run
uniform with (seed = 1) = [ 0.23903739]
uniform with (seed = 1) = [ 0.22267115]
uniform without seed = [ 0.50188708]
uniform without seed = [ 0.21324408]
>>>
```

# Montecarlo's method

We end the section on random numbers with a simple note about the Montecarlo method. It is a numerical probabilistic method widely used in the application of high-performance scientific computing. In our example, we will calculate the value of π:

```
import TensorFlow as tf

trials = 100
hits = 0
```

Generate pseudo-random points inside the square $[-1, 1] \times [-1, 1]$, using the `random_uniform` function:

```
x = tf.random_uniform([1],minval=-1,maxval=1,dtype=tf.float32)
y = tf.random_uniform([1],minval=-1,maxval=1,dtype=tf.float32)
pi = []
```

Start the session:

```
sess = tf.Session()
```

Inside the session, we calculate the value of π: the area of the circle is π and that of the square is 4. The relationship between the numbers inside the circle and the total of generated points must converge (very slowly) to π, and we count how many points fall inside the circle equation $x^2+y^2=1$.

```
with sess.as_default():
    for i in range(1,trials):
        for j in range(1,trials):
            if x.eval()**2 + y.eval()**2 < 1 :
                hits = hits + 1
                pi.append((4 * float(hits) / i)/trials)

plt.plot(pi)
plt.show()
```

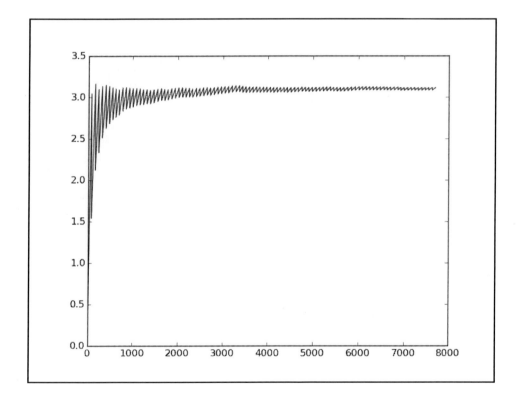

The figure shows the convergence during the number of tests to the π value

# Solving partial differential equations

A **partial differential equation** (**PDE**) is a differential equation involving partial derivatives of an unknown function of several independent variables. PDEs are commonly used to formulate and solve major physical problems in various fields, from quantum mechanics to financial markets. In this section, we take the example from `https://www.TensorFlow.or g/versions/r0.8/tutorials/pdes/index.html`, showing the use of TensorFlow in a two-dimensional PDE solution that models the surface of square pond with a few raindrops landing on it. The effect will be to produce bi-dimensional waves on the pond itself. We won't concentrate on the computational aspects of the problem, as this is beyond the scope of this book; instead we will focus on using TensorFlow to define the problem.

The starting point is to import these fundamental libraries:

```
import TensorFlow as tf
import numpy as np
import matplotlib.pyplot as plt
```

# Initial condition

First we have to define the dimensions of the problem. Let's imagine that our pond is a 500×500 square:

```
N = 500
```

The following two-dimensional tensor is the pond at time `t = 0`, that is, the *initial condition* of our problem:

```
u_init = np.zeros([N, N], dtype=np.float32)
```

We have 40 random raindrops on it

```
for n in range(40):
  a,b = np.random.randint(0, N, 2)
  u_init[a,b] = np.random.uniform()
```

The `np.random.randint(0, N, 2)` is a NumPy function that returns random integers from 0 to N on a two-dimensional shape.

Using matplotlib, we can show the initial square pond:

```
plt.imshow(U.eval())
plt.show()
```

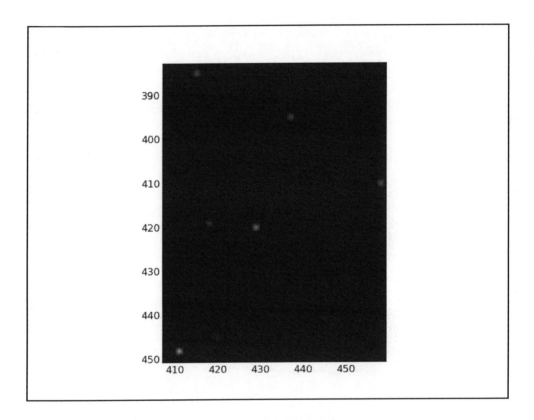

Zooming on the pond in its initial condition: the colored dots represent the raindrops fallen

Then we define the following tensor:

```
ut_init = np.zeros([N, N], dtype=np.float32)
```

It is the *temporal evolution* of the pond. At time $t = t_{end}$ it will contain the final state of the pond.

# Model building

We must define some fundamental parameters (using TensorFlow placeholders) and a time step of the simulation:

```
eps = tf.placeholder(tf.float32, shape=())
```

We must also define a physical parameter of the model, namely the `damping` coefficient:

```
damping = tf.placeholder(tf.float32, shape=())
```

Then we redefine our starting tensors as TensorFlow variables, since their values will change over the course of the simulation:

```
U  = tf.Variable(u_init)
Ut = tf.Variable(ut_init)
```

Finally, we build our PDE model. It represents the evolution in time of the pond after the raindrops have fallen:

```
U_  = U + eps * Ut
Ut_ = Ut + eps * (laplace(U) – damping * Ut)
```

As you can see, we introduced the `laplace(U)` function to resolve the PDE (it will be described in the last part of this section).

Using the TensorFlow group operator, we define how our pond in time `t` should evolve:

```
step = tf.group(
 U.assign(U_),
 Ut.assign(Ut_))
```

Let's recall that the group operator groups multiple operations as a single one.

# Graph execution

In our session we will see the evolution in time of the pond by `1000` steps, where each time step is equal to `0.03s`, while the damping coefficient is set equal to `0.04`.

Let's initialize the TensorFlow variables:

```
tf.initialize_all_variables().run()
```

Then we run the simulation:

```
for i in range(1000):
  step.run({eps: 0.03, damping: 0.04})
  if i % 50 == 0:
    clear_output()
    plt.imshow(U.eval())
    plt.show()
```

Every 50 steps the simulation result will be displayed as follows:

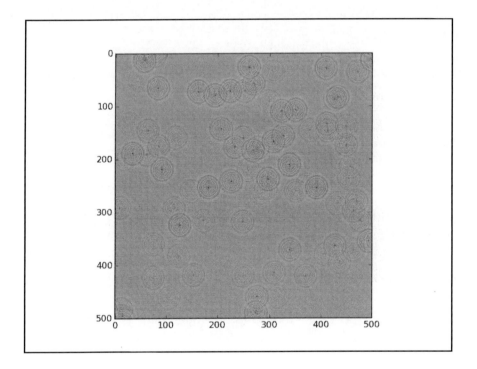

The pond after 400 simulation steps

# Computational function used

Let's now see what is the `Laplace(U)` function and the ancillary functions used:

```
def make_kernel(a):
  a = np.asarray(a)
  a = a.reshape(list(a.shape) + [1,1])
  return tf.constant(a, dtype=1)
```

```
def simple_conv(x, k):
  x = tf.expand_dims(tf.expand_dims(x, 0), -1)
  y = tf.nn.depthwise_conv2d(x, k, [1, 1, 1, 1],padding='SAME')
  return y[0, :, :, 0]

def laplace(x):
    laplace_k = make_kernel([[0.5, 1.0, 0.5],
                             [1.0, -6., 1.0],
                             [0.5, 1.0, 0.5]])
    return simple_conv(x, laplace_k)
```

These functions describe the physics of the model, that is, as the wave is created and propagates in the pond. I will not go into the details of these functions, the understanding of which is beyond the scope of this book.

The following figure shows the waves on the pond after the raindrops have fallen.

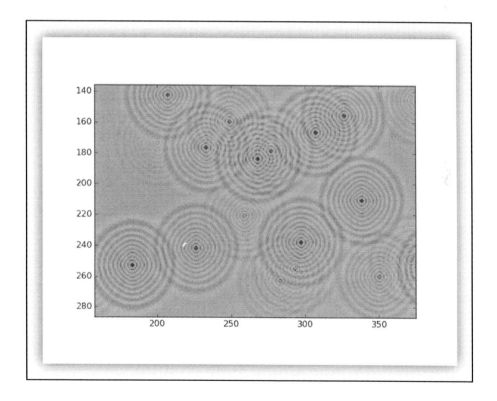

Zooming on the pond

# Summary

In this chapter, we looked at some of the mathematical potential of TensorFlow. From the fundamental definition of a *tensor*, the basic data structure for any type of computation, we saw with some examples how to handle these data structures using the TensorFlow's math operators. Using *complex* numbers, we explored the world of fractals. Then we introduced the concept of *random* numbers. These are in fact used in machine learning for model development and testing, so the chapter ended with an example of defining and solving a mathematical problem using differential equations with partial derivatives.

In the next chapter, finally we'll start to see TensorFlow in action right in the field for which it was developed – in machine learning, solving complex problems such as *classification* and *data clustering*.

# 3
# Starting with Machine Learning

In this chapter, we will cover the following topics:

- Linear regression
- The MNIST dataset
- Classifiers
- The nearest neighbor algorithm
- Data clustering
- The k-means algorithm

## The linear regression algorithm

In this section, we begin our exploration of machine learning techniques with the linear regression algorithm. Our goal is to build a model by which to predict the values of a dependent variable from the values of one or more independent variables.

The relationship between these two variables is linear; that is, if $y$ is the dependent variable and $x$ the independent, then the linear relationship between the two variables will look like this: $y = Ax + b$.

The linear regression algorithm adapts to a great variety of situations; for its versatility, it is used extensively in the field of applied sciences, for example, biology and economics.

Furthermore, the implementation of this algorithm allows us to introduce in a totally clear and understandable way the two important concepts of machine learning: **the cost function** and the **gradient descent algorithms**.

# Data model

The first crucial step is to build our data model. We mentioned earlier that the relationship between our variables is linear, that is: $y = Ax + b$, where A and b are constants. To test our algorithm, we need data points in a two-dimensional space.

We start by importing the Python library NumPy:

```
import numpy as np
```

Then we define the number of points we want to draw:

```
number_of_points = 500
```

We initialize the following two lists:

```
x_point = []
y_point = []
```

These points will contain the generated points.

We then set the two constants that will appear in the linear relation of y with x:

```
a = 0.22
b = 0.78
```

Via NumPy's `random.normal` function, we generate 300 random points around the regression equation $y = 0.22x + 0.78$:

```
for i in range(number_of_points):
    x = np.random.normal(0.0,0.5)
    y = a*x + b +np.random.normal(0.0,0.1)
    x_point.append([x])
    y_point.append([y])
```

Finally, view the generated points by `matplotlib`:

```
import matplotlib.pyplot as plt
plt.plot(x_point,y_point, 'o', label='Input Data')
plt.legend()
plt.show()
```

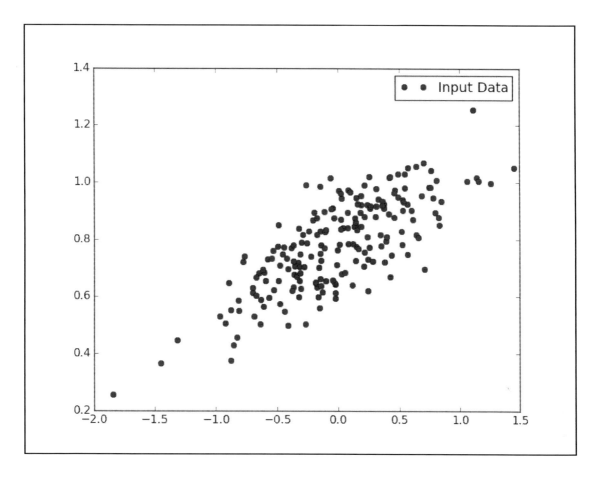

Linear regression: The data model

# Cost functions and gradient descent

The machine learning algorithm that we want to implement with TensorFlow must predict values of y as a function of x data according to our data model. The linear regression algorithm will determine the values of the constants A and b (fixed for our data model), which are then the true unknowns of the problem.

The first step is to import the tensorflow library:

```
import tensorflow as tf
```

Then define the A and b unknowns, using the TensorFlow tf.Variable:

```
A = tf.Variable(tf.random_uniform([1], -1.0, 1.0))
```

The unknown factor A was initialized using a random value between -1 and 1, while the variable b is initially set to zero:

```
b = tf.Variable(tf.zeros([1]))
```

So we write the linear relationship that binds y to x:

```
y = A * x_point + b
```

Now we will introduce, this *cost function*: that has parameters containing a pair of values A and b to be determined which returns a value that estimates how well the parameters are correct. In this example, our cost function is *mean square error*:

```
cost_function = tf.reduce_mean(tf.square(y - y_point))
```

It provides an estimate of the variability of the measures, or more precisely, of the dispersion of values around the average value; a small value of this function corresponds to a best estimate for the unknown parameters A and b.

To minimize cost_function, we use an optimization algorithm with the *gradient descent*. Given a mathematical function of several variables, gradient descent allows to find a local minimum of this function. The technique is as follows:

- **Evaluate**, at an arbitrary first point of the function's domain, the function itself and its gradient. The gradient indicates the direction in which the function tends to a minimum.
- **Select** a second point in the direction indicated by the gradient. If the function for this second point has a value lower than the value calculated at the first point, the descent can continue.

You can refer to the following figure for a visual explanation of the algorithm:

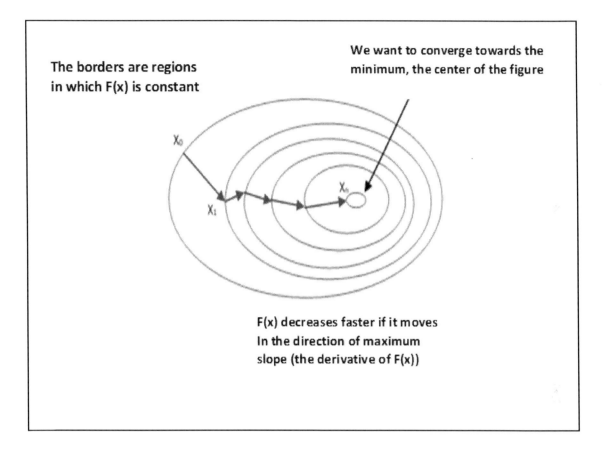

The gradient descent algorithm

We also remark that the gradient descent is only a *local function minimum*, but it can also be used in the search for a global minimum, randomly choosing a new start point once it has found a local minimum and repeating the process many times. If the number of minima of the function is limited, and there are very high number of attempts, then there is a good chance that sooner or later the global minimum will be identified.

Using TensorFlow, the application of this algorithm is very simple. The instruction are as follows:

```
optimizer = tf.train.GradientDescentOptimizer(0.5)
```

Here 0.5 is the *learning rate* of the algorithm.

The learning rate determines how fast or slow we move towards the optimal weights. If it is very large, we skip the optimal solution, and if it is too small, we need too many iterations to converge to the best values.

An intermediate value (0.5) is provided, but it must be tuned in order to improve the performance of the entire procedure.

We define train as the result of the application of the cost_function (optimizer), through its minimize function:

```
train = optimizer.minimize(cost_function)
```

## Testing the model

Now we can test the algorithm of gradient descent on the data model you created earlier. As usual, we have to initialize all the variables:

```
model = tf.initialize_all_variables()
```

So we build our iteration (20 computation steps), allowing us to determine the best values of A and b, which define the line that best fits the data model. Instantiate the evaluation graph:

```
with tf.Session() as session:
```

We perform the simulation on our model:

```
session.run(model)
for step in range(0,21):
```

For each iteration, we execute the optimization step:

```
session.run(train)
```

Every five steps, we print our pattern of dots:

```
if (step % 5) == 0:
    plt.plot(x_point,y_point,'o',
             label='step = {}'
             .format(step))
```

And the straight lines are obtained by the following command:

```
plt.plot(x_point,
         session.run(A) *
         x_point +
         session.run(B))
plt.legend()
plt.show()
```

The following figure shows the convergence of the implemented algorithm:

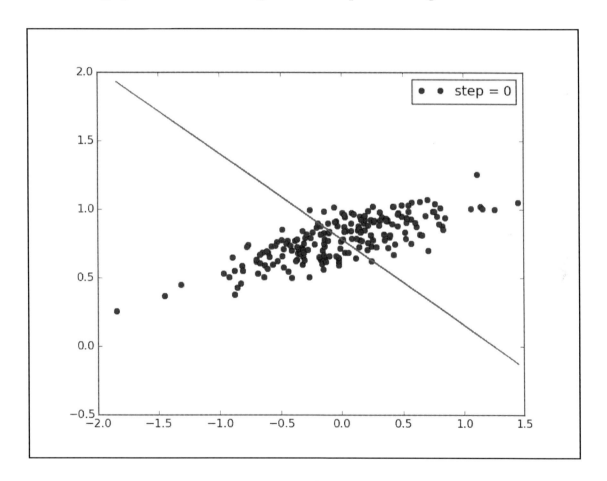

Linear regression : start computation (step = 0)

After just five steps, we can already see (in the next figure) a substantial improvement in the fit of the line:

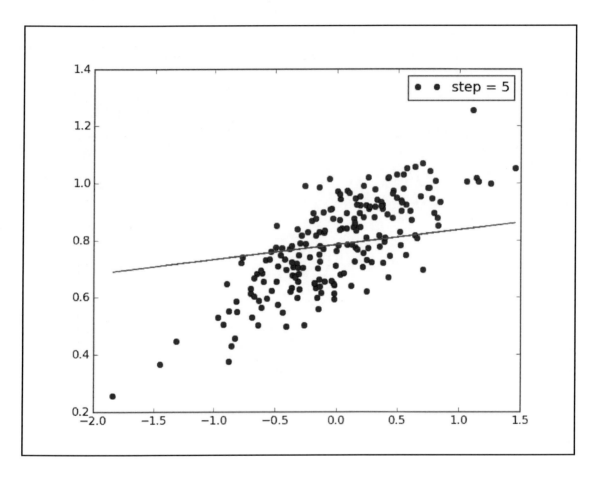

Linear regression: situation after 5 computation steps

The following (and final) figure shows the definitive result after 20 steps. We can see the efficiency of the algorithm used, with the straight line efficiency perfectly across the cloud of points.

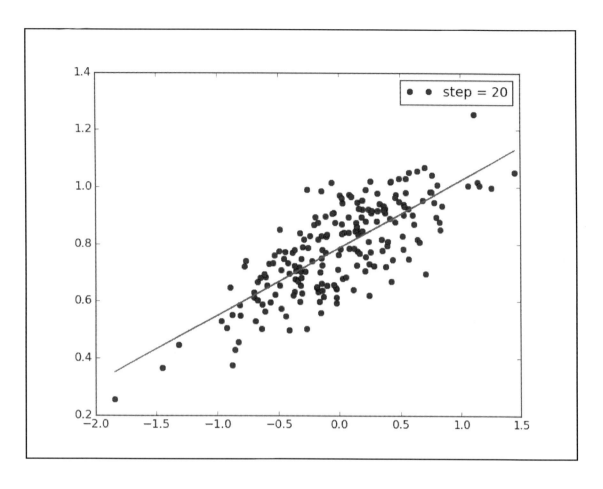

Linear regression: final result

Finally we report, to further our understanding, the complete code:

```python
import numpy as np
import matplotlib.pyplot as plt
import tensorflow as tf
number_of_points = 200
x_point = []
y_point = []
a = 0.22
b = 0.78
for i in range(number_of_points):
    x = np.random.normal(0.0,0.5)
    y = a*x + b +np.random.normal(0.0,0.1)
```

```
    x_point.append([x])
    y_point.append([y])
plt.plot(x_point,y_point, 'o', label='Input Data')
plt.legend()
plt.show()
A = tf.Variable(tf.random_uniform([1], -1.0, 1.0))
B = tf.Variable(tf.zeros([1]))
y = A * x_point + B
cost_function = tf.reduce_mean(tf.square(y - y_point))
optimizer = tf.train.GradientDescentOptimizer(0.5)
train = optimizer.minimize(cost_function)
model = tf.initialize_all_variables()
with tf.Session() as session:
        session.run(model)
        for step in range(0,21):
                session.run(train)
                if (step % 5) == 0:
                        plt.plot(x_point,y_point,'o',
                                label='step = {}'
                                .format(step))
                        plt.plot(x_point,
                                session.run(A) *
                                x_point +
                                session.run(B))
                        plt.legend()
                        plt.show()
```

# The MNIST dataset

The MNIST dataset (available at `http://yann.lecun.com/exdb/mnist/`), is widely used for training and testing in the field of machine learning, and we will use it in the examples of this book. It contains black and white images of handwritten digits from 0 to 9.

The data set is divided into two groups: 60,000 to train the model and an additional 10,000 to test it. The original images, in black and white, were normalized to fit into a box of size 28×28 pixels and centered by calculating the center of mass of the pixels. The following figure represents how the digits could be represented in the MNIST dataset:

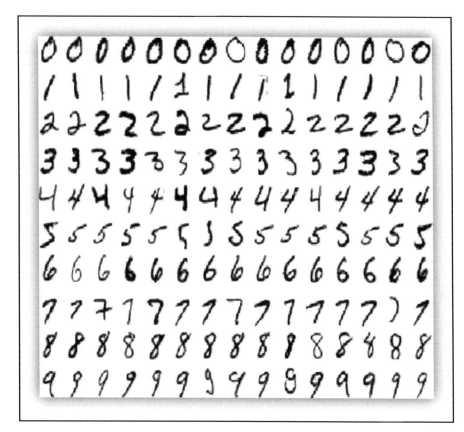

MNIST digit sampling

Each MNIST data point is an array of numbers describing how dark each pixel is. For example, for the following digit (the digit 1), we could have:

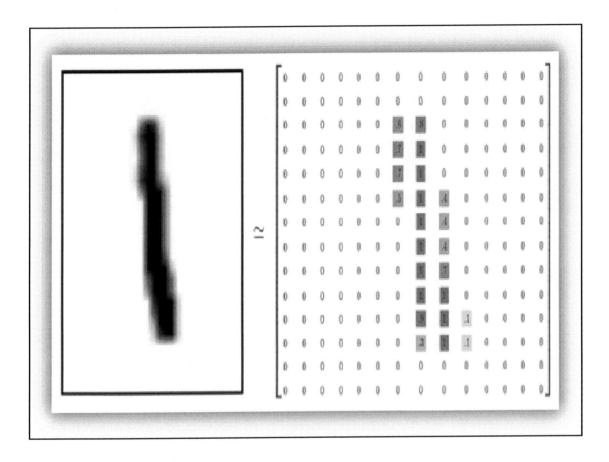

Pixel representation of the digit 1

# Downloading and preparing the data

The following code imports the MNIST data files that we are going to classify. I am using a script from Google that can be downloaded from:

https://github.com/tensorflow/tensorflow/blob/r0.7/tensorflow/examples/tutorials/mnist/input_data.py. This must be run in the same folder where the files are located.

Now we will show how to load and display the data:

```
import input_data
import numpy as np
import matplotlib.pyplot as plt
```

Using input_data, we load the data sets:

```
mnist_images = input_data.read_data_sets\
               ("MNIST_data/",\
                one_hot=False)
train.next_batch(10) returns the first 10 images :
pixels,real_values = mnist_images.train.next_batch(10)
```

This also returns two lists: the matrix of the pixels loaded and the list that contains the real values loaded:

```
print "list of values loaded ",real_values
example_to_visualize = 5
print "element N° " + str(example_to_visualize + 1)\
                    + " of the list plotted"
>>
Extracting MNIST_data/train-labels-idx1-ubyte.gz
Extracting MNIST_data/t10k-images-idx3-ubyte.gz
Extracting MNIST_data/t10k-labels-idx1-ubyte.gz
list of values loaded   [7 3 4 6 1 8 1 0 9 8]
element N 6 of the list plotted
>>
```

While displaying an element, we can use matplotlib, as follows:

```
image = pixels[example_to_visualize,:]
image = np.reshape(image,[28,28])
plt.imshow(image)
plt.show()
```

Here is the result:

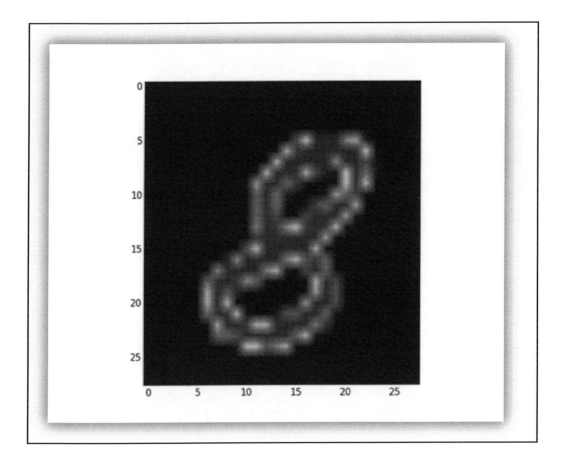

A MNIST image of the number eight

# Classifiers

In the context of machine learning, the term *classification* identifies an algorithmic procedure that assigns each new input datum (*instance*) to one of the possible categories (*classes*). If we consider only two classes, we talk about binary classification; otherwise we have a multi-class classification.

The classification falls into the *supervised learning* category, which permits us to classify new instances based on the so-called *training set*. The basic steps to follow to resolve a supervised classification problem are as follows:

1. Build the training examples in order to represent the actual context and application on which to accomplish the classification.
2. Choose the classifier and the corresponding algorithm implementation.
3. Train the algorithm on the training set and set any control parameters through validation.
4. Evaluate the accuracy and performance of the classifier by applying a set of new instances (test set).

# The nearest neighbor algorithm

The **K-nearest neighbor** (**KNN**) is a supervised learning algorithm for both classification or regression. It is a system that assigns the class of the sample tested according to its distance from the objects stored in the memory.

The distance, d, is defined as the Euclidean distance between two points:

$$d = \sqrt{\sum_{i=1}^{n} (x_i - y_i)^2}$$

Here n is the dimension of the space. The advantage of this method of classification is the ability to classify objects whose classes *are not linearly separable*. It is a stable classifier, given that *small perturbations* of the training data *do not significantly affect* the results obtained. The most obvious disadvantage, however, is that it does not provide a true mathematical model; instead, for every new classification, it should be carried out by adding the new data to all initial instances and repeating the calculation procedure for the selected K value.

Moreover, it requires a fairly high amount of data to make realistic predictions and is sensitive to the noise of the analyzed data.

In the next example, we will implement the KNNalgorithm using the MNIST data set.

# Building the training set

Let's start with the import libraries needed for the simulation:

```
import numpy as np
import tensorflow as tf
import input_data
```

To construct the data model for the training set, use the `input_data.read_data_sets` function, introduced earlier:

```
mnist = input_data.read_data_sets("/tmp/data/", one_hot=True)
```

In our example we will take training phase consisting of 100 MNIST images:

```
train_pixels,train_list_values = mnist.train.next_batch(100)
```

While we test our algorithm for 10 images:

```
test_pixels,test_list_of_values  = mnist.test.next_batch(10)
```

Finally, we define the tensors `train_pixel_tensor` and `test_pixel_tensor` we use to construct our classifier:

```
train_pixel_tensor = tf.placeholder\
                        ("float", [None, 784])
test_pixel_tensor = tf.placeholder\
                        ("float", [784])
```

# Cost function and optimization

The cost function is represented by the distance in terms of pixels:

```
distance = tf.reduce_sum\
            (tf.abs\
            (tf.add(train_pixel_tensor, \
                    tf.neg(test_pixel_tensor))), \
            reduction_indices=1)
```

The `tf.reduce` function sum computes the sum of elements across the dimensions of a tensor. For example (from the TensorFlow on-line manual):

```
# 'x' is [[1, 1, 1]
#         [1, 1, 1]]
tf.reduce_sum(x) ==> 6
tf.reduce_sum(x, 0) ==> [2, 2, 2]
tf.reduce_sum(x, 1) ==> [3, 3]
tf.reduce_sum(x, 1, keep_dims=True) ==> [[3], [3]]
tf.reduce_sum(x, [0, 1]) ==> 6
```

Finally, to minimize the distance function, we use `arg_min`, which returns the index with the smallest distance (nearest neighbor):

```
pred = tf.arg_min(distance, 0)
```

## Testing and algorithm evaluation

Accuracy is a parameter that helps us to compute the final result of the classifier:

```
accuracy = 0
```

Initialize the variables:

```
init = tf.initialize_all_variables()
```

Start the simulation:

```
with tf.Session() as sess:
    sess.run(init)
    for i in range(len(test_list_of_values)):
```

Then we evaluate the nearest neighbor index, using the `pred` function, defined earlier:

```
nn_index = sess.run(pred, \
    feed_dict={train_pixel_tensor:train_pixels, \
    test_pixel_tensor:test_pixels[i,:]})
```

Finally, we find the nearest neighbor class label and compare it to its true label:

```
        print "Test N° ", i,"Predicted Class: ", \
    np.argmax(train_list_values[nn_index]),\
    "True Class: ", np.argmax(test_list_of_values[i])
        if np.argmax(train_list_values[nn_index])\
    == np.argmax(test_list_of_values[i]):
```

Then we evaluate and report the accuracy of the classifier:

```
              accuracy += 1./len(test_pixels)
      print "Result = ", accuracy
```

As we can see, each element of the training set is correctly classified. The result of the simulation shows the predicted class with the real class, and finally the total value of the simulation is reported:

```
>>>
Extracting /tmp/data/train-labels-idx1-ubyte.gz
Extracting /tmp/data/t10k-images-idx3-ubyte.gz
Extracting /tmp/data/t10k-labels-idx1-ubyte.gz
Test N°  0 Predicted Class:  7 True Class:  7
Test N°  1 Predicted Class:  2 True Class:  2
Test N°  2 Predicted Class:  1 True Class:  1
Test N°  3 Predicted Class:  0 True Class:  0
Test N°  4 Predicted Class:  4 True Class:  4
Test N°  5 Predicted Class:  1 True Class:  1
Test N°  6 Predicted Class:  4 True Class:  4
Test N°  7 Predicted Class:  9 True Class:  9
Test N°  8 Predicted Class:  6 True Class:  5
Test N°  9 Predicted Class:  9 True Class:  9
Result =  0.9
>>>
```

The result is not 100% accurate; the reason is that it lies in a wrong evaluation of the test no. 8 instead of 5, the classifier has rated 6.

Finally, we report the complete code for KNN classification:

```
import numpy as np
import tensorflow as tf
import input_data
#Build the Training Set

mnist = input_data.read_data_sets("/tmp/data/", one_hot=True)
train_pixels,train_list_values = mnist.train.next_batch(100)
test_pixels,test_list_of_values  = mnist.test.next_batch(10)
train_pixel_tensor = tf.placeholder\
                    ("float", [None, 784])
test_pixel_tensor = tf.placeholder\
                    ("float", [784])
#Cost Function and distance optimization
distance = tf.reduce_sum\
            (tf.abs\
             (tf.add(train_pixel_tensor, \
                    tf.neg(test_pixel_tensor))), \
```

```
                    reduction_indices=1)
pred = tf.arg_min(distance, 0)
# Testing and algorithm evaluation
accuracy = 0.
init = tf.initialize_all_variables()
with tf.Session() as sess:
    sess.run(init)
    for i in range(len(test_list_of_values)):
        nn_index = sess.run(pred,\
    feed_dict={train_pixel_tensor:train_pixels,\
    test_pixel_tensor:test_pixels[i,:]})
        print "Test N° ", i,"Predicted Class: ", \
    np.argmax(train_list_values[nn_index]),\
    "True Class: ", np.argmax(test_list_of_values[i])
        if np.argmax(train_list_values[nn_index])\
    == np.argmax(test_list_of_values[i]):
            accuracy += 1./len(test_pixels)
    print "Result = ", accuracy
```

# Data clustering

A clustering problem consists in the selection and grouping of homogeneous items from a set of initial data. To solve this problem, we must:

- Identify a *resemblance* measure between elements
- Find out if there are subsets of elements that are *similar* to the measure chosen

The algorithm determines which elements form a cluster and what degree of similarity unites them within the cluster.

The clustering algorithms fall into the *unsupervised methods*, because we do not assume any prior information on the structures and characteristics of the clusters.

# The k-means algorithm

One of the most common and simple *clustering algorithms* is k-means, which allows subdividing groups of objects into k partitions on the basis of their attributes. Each cluster is identified by a *point* or *centroid average*.

The algorithm follows an iterative procedure:

1. Randomly select K points as the initial centroids.
2. Repeat.
3. Form K clusters by assigning all points to the closest centroid.
4. Recompute the centroid of each cluster.
5. Until the centroids don't change.

The popularity of the k-means comes from its *convergence speed* and its *ease of implementation*. In terms of the quality of the solutions, the algorithm does not guarantee achieving the global optimum. The quality of the final solution *depends* largely on the *initial set* of clusters and may, in practice, to obtain a much worse the global optimum solution. Since the algorithm is extremely fast, you can apply it several times and produce solutions from which you can choose among most satisfying one. Another disadvantage of the algorithm is that it requires you to choose the number of clusters (k) to find.

If the data is not naturally partitioned, you will end up getting strange results. Furthermore, the algorithm works well only when there are identifiable spherical clusters in the data.

Let us now see how to implement the k-means by the TensorFlow library.

# Building the training set

Import all the necessary libraries to our simulation:

```
import matplotlib.pyplot as plt
import numpy as np
import tensorflow as tf
import pandas as pd
```

 Pandas is an open source, easy-to-use data structure, and data analysis tool for the Python programming language. To install it, type the following command:

```
sudo pip install pandas
```

We must define the parameters of our problem. The total number of points that we want to cluster is 1000 points:

```
num_vectors = 1000
```

The number of partitions you want to achieve by all initial:

```
num_clusters = 4
```

We set the number of computational steps of the k-means algorithm:

```
num_steps = 100
```

We initialize the initial input data structures:

```
x_values = []
y_values = []
vector_values = []
```

The *training set* creates a random set of points, which is why we use the random.normal NumPy function, allowing us to build the x_values and y_values vectors:

```
for i in xrange(num_vectors):
  if np.random.random() > 0.5:
    x_values.append(np.random.normal(0.4, 0.7))
    y_values.append(np.random.normal(0.2, 0.8))
  else:
    x_values.append(np.random.normal(0.6, 0.4))
    y_values.append(np.random.normal(0.8, 0.5))
```

We use the Python zip function to obtain the complete list of vector_values:

```
vector_values = zip(x_values,y_values)
```

Then vector_values is converted into a constant, usable by TensorFlow:

```
vectors = tf.constant(vector_values)
```

We can see our *training set* for the clustering algorithm with the following commands:

```
plt.plot(x_values,y_values, 'o', label='Input Data')
plt.legend()
plt.show()
```

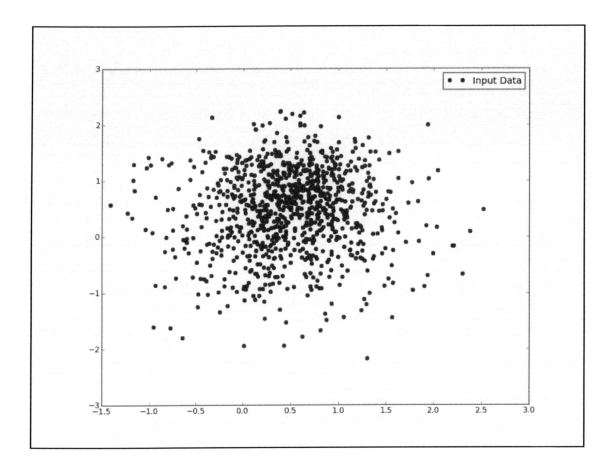

The training set for k-means

After randomly building the training set, we have to generate ($k = 4$) centroid, then determine an index using `tf.random_shuffle`:

```
n_samples = tf.shape(vector_values)[0]
random_indices = tf.random_shuffle(tf.range(0, n_samples))
```

By adopting this procedure, we are able to determine four random indices:

```
begin = [0,]
size = [num_clusters,]
size[0] = num_clusters
```

They have their own indexes of our initial centroids:

```
centroid_indices = tf.slice(random_indices, begin, size)
centroids = tf.Variable(tf.gather\
            (vector_values, centroid_indices))
```

# Cost functions and optimization

The cost function we want to minimize for this problem is again the Euclidean distance between two points:

$$d = \sqrt{\sum_{i=1}^{n} (x_i - y_i)^2}$$

In order to manage the tensors defined previously, `vectors` and `centroids`, we use the TensorFlow function `expand_dims`, which automatically expands the size of the two arguments:

```
expanded_vectors = tf.expand_dims(vectors, 0)
expanded_centroids = tf.expand_dims(centroids, 1)
```

This function allows you to standardize the shape of the two tensors, in order to evaluate the difference by the `tf.sub` method:

```
vectors_subtration = tf.sub(expanded_vectors, expanded_centroids)
```

Finally, we build the `euclidean_distances` cost function, using the `tf.reduce_sum` function, which computes the sum of elements across the dimensions of a tensor, while the `tf.square` function computes the square of the `vectors_subtration` element-wise tensor:

```
euclidean_distances = tf.reduce_sum(tf.square\
                            (vectors_subtration), 2)
assignments = tf.to_int32(tf.argmin(euclidean_distances, 0))
```

Here `assignments` is the value of the index with the smallest distance across the tensor `euclidean_distances`. Let us now turn to the optimization phase, the purpose of which is to improve the choice of centroids, on which the construction of the clusters depends. We partition the `vectors` (which is our *training set*) into `num_clusters` tensors, using indices from `assignments`.

The following code takes the nearest indices for each sample, and grabs those out as separate groups using `tf.dynamic_partition`:

```
partitions = tf.dynamic_partition\
             (vectors, assignments, num_clusters)
```

Finally, we update the centroids, using `tf.reduce_mean` on a single group to find the average of that group, forming its new centroid:

```
update_centroids = tf.concat(0, \
                                [tf.expand_dims\
                            (tf.reduce_mean(partition, 0), 0)\
                                for partition in partitions])
```

To form the `update_centroids` tensor, we use `tf.concat` to concatenate the single one.

# Testing and algorithm evaluation

It's time to test and evaluate the algorithm. The first procedure is to initialize all the variables and instantiate the evaluation graph:

```
init_op = tf.initialize_all_variables()
sess = tf.Session()
sess.run(init_op)
```

Now we start the computation:

```
for step in xrange(num_steps):
    _, centroid_values, assignment_values =\
        sess.run([update_centroids,\
                    centroids,\
                    assignments])
```

To display the result, we implement the following function:

```
display_partition(x_values,y_values,assignment_values)
```

This takes the `x_values` and `y_values` vectors of the training set, and the `assignemnt_values` vector, to draw the clusters.

The code for this visualization function is as follows:

```
def display_partition(x_values,y_values,assignment_values):
    labels = []
    colors = ["red","blue","green","yellow"]
    for i in xrange(len(assignment_values)):
        labels.append(colors[(assignment_values[i])])
    color = labels
    df = pd.DataFrame\
        (dict(x =x_values,y = y_values ,color = labels ))
    fig, ax = plt.subplots()
    ax.scatter(df['x'], df['y'], c=df['color'])
    plt.show()
```

It associates to each cluster its color by means of the following data structure:

```
colors = ["red","blue","green","yellow"]
```

It then draws them through the `scatter` function of matplotlib:

```
ax.scatter(df['x'], df['y'], c=df['color'])
```

Let's display the result:

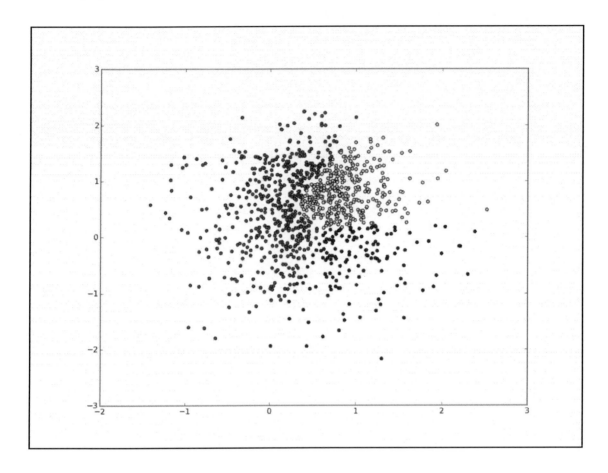

Final result of the k-means algorithm

Here is the complete code of the k-means algorithm:

```
import matplotlib.pyplot as plt
import numpy as np
import pandas as pd
import tensorflow as tf
def display_partition(x_values,y_values,assignment_values):
    labels = []
    colors = ["red","blue","green","yellow"]
    for i in xrange(len(assignment_values)):
      labels.append(colors[(assignment_values[i])])
    color = labels
```

```
        df = pd.DataFrame\
                (dict(x =x_values,y = y_values ,color = labels ))
        fig, ax = plt.subplots()
        ax.scatter(df['x'], df['y'], c=df['color'])
        plt.show()
    num_vectors = 2000
    num_clusters = 4
    n_samples_per_cluster = 500
    num_steps = 1000
    x_values = []
    y_values = []
    vector_values = []
    #CREATE RANDOM DATA
    for i in xrange(num_vectors):
      if np.random.random() > 0.5:
        x_values.append(np.random.normal(0.4, 0.7))
        y_values.append(np.random.normal(0.2, 0.8))
      else:
        x_values.append(np.random.normal(0.6, 0.4))
        y_values.append(np.random.normal(0.8, 0.5))
    vector_values = zip(x_values,y_values)
    vectors = tf.constant(vector_values)
    n_samples = tf.shape(vector_values)[0]
    random_indices = tf.random_shuffle(tf.range(0, n_samples))
    begin = [0,]
    size = [num_clusters,]
    size[0] = num_clusters
    centroid_indices = tf.slice(random_indices, begin, size)
    centroids = tf.Variable(tf.gather(vector_values, centroid_indices))
    expanded_vectors = tf.expand_dims(vectors, 0)
    expanded_centroids = tf.expand_dims(centroids, 1)
    vectors_subtration = tf.sub(expanded_vectors,expanded_centroids)
    euclidean_distances =
                  \tf.reduce_sum(tf.square(vectors_subtration), 2)
    assignments = tf.to_int32(tf.argmin(euclidean_distances, 0))
    partitions = [0, 0, 1, 1, 0]
    num_partitions = 2
    data = [10, 20, 30, 40, 50]
    outputs[0] = [10, 20, 50]
    outputs[1] = [30, 40]
    partitions = tf.dynamic_partition(vectors, assignments, num_clusters)
    update_centroids = tf.concat(0, [tf.expand_dims
(tf.reduce_mean(partition, 0), 0)\
                              for partition in partitions])
    init_op = tf.initialize_all_variables()
    sess = tf.Session()
    sess.run(init_op)
    for step in xrange(num_steps):
```

```
    _, centroid_values, assignment_values =\
       sess.run([update_centroids,\
                 centroids,\
                 assignments])
display_partition(x_values,y_values,assignment_values)
plt.plot(x_values,y_values, 'o', label='Input Data')
plt.legend()
plt.show()
```

# Summary

In this chapter, we began to explore the potential of TensorFlow for some typical problems in Machine Learning. With the *linear regression* algorithm, the important concepts of *cost function* and optimization using *gradient descent* were explained. We then described the dataset MNIST of handwritten digits. We also implemented a multiclass classifier using the *nearest neighbor* algorithm, which falls into the Machine Learning *supervised learning* category. Then the chapter concluded with an example of *unsupervised learning*, by implementing the k-means algorithm for solving a data clustering problem.

In the next chapter, we will introduce neural networks. These are mathematical models that represent the interconnection between elements defined as *artificial neurons*, namely mathematical constructs that mimic the properties of living neurons.

We'll also implement some neural network learning models using TensorFlow.

# 4
# Introducing Neural Networks

In this chapter, we will cover the following topics:

- What are neural networks?
- Single Layer Perceptron
- Logistic regression
- Multi Layer Perceptron
- Multi Layer Perceptron classification
- Multi Layer Perceptron function approximation

## What are artificial neural networks?

An **artificial neural network** (**ANN**) is an information processing system whose operating mechanism is inspired by biological neural circuits. Thanks to their characteristics, neural networks are the protagonists of a real revolution in machine learning systems and more specifically in the context of artificial intelligence. An ANN possesses many simple processing units variously connected to each other, according to various architectures. If we look at the schema of an ANN reported later, it can be seen that the *hidden units* communicate with the external layer, both in input and output, while the *input* and *output units* communicate only with the *hidden layer* of the network.

Each unit or node simulates the role of the neuron in biological neural networks. Each node, said *artificial neuron*, has a very simple operation: it becomes active if the total quantity of signal that it receives exceeds its activation threshold, defined by the so-called activation function. If a node *becomes active*, it emits a signal that is transmitted along the transmission channels up to the other unit to which it is connected. Each connection point acts as a filter that converts the message into an inhibitory or excitatory signal, increasing or decreasing the intensity according to their individual characteristics. The connection points simulate the biological synapses and have the fundamental function of weighing the intensity of the transmitted signals, by multiplying them by the weights whose values depend on the connection itself.

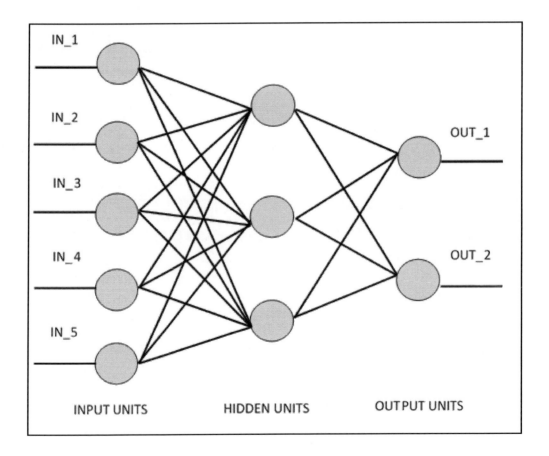

ANN schematic diagram

# Neural network architectures

The *way to connect* the nodes, the *total number* of layers, that is the levels of nodes between input and outputs and the number of neurons per layer-all these define the *architecture* of a neural network. For example, in **multilayer networks** (we introduce these in the second part of this chapter), one can identify the artificial neurons of layers such that:

- Each neuron is connected with all those of the next layer
- There are no connections between neurons belonging to the same layer
- The number of layers and of neurons per layer depends on the problem to be solved

Now we start our exploration of neural network models, introducing the most simple neural network model: the Single Layer Perceptron or the so-called Rosenblatt's Perceptron.

# Single Layer Perceptron

The Single Layer Perceptron was the first neural network model, proposed in 1958 by Frank Rosenblatt. In this model, the content of the local memory of the neuron consists of a vector of weights, `W = (w1, w2, ......, wn)`. The computation is performed over the calculation of a sum of the input vector `X = (x1, x2, ......, xn)`, each of which is multiplied by the corresponding element of the vector of the weights; then the value provided in the output (that is, a weighted sum) will be the input of an activation function. This function returns `1` if the result is greater than a certain threshold, otherwise it returns `-1`. In the following figure, the activation function is the so-called `sign` function:

```
                +1          x > 0
    sign(x)= -1             otherwise
```

It is possible to use other activation functions, preferably non-linear (such as the `sigmoid` function, which we will see in the next section). The learning procedure of the net is iterative: it slightly modifies for each learning cycle (called epoch) the synaptic weights by using a selected set called a training set. At each cycle, the weights must be modified to minimize a cost function, which is specific to the problem under consideration. Finally, when the perceptron has been trained on the training set, it will be tested on other inputs (the test set) in order to verify its capacity for generalization.

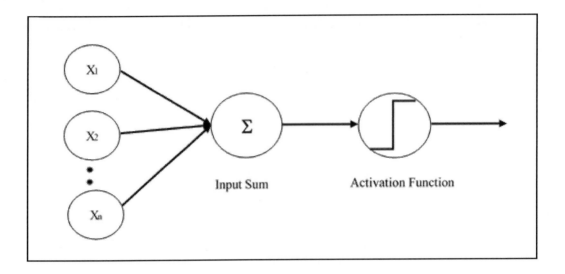

Schema of a Rosemblatt's Perceptron

Let us now see how to implement a single layer neural network for an image classification problem using TensorFlow.

# The logistic regression

This algorithm has nothing to do with the canonical linear regression we saw in `Chapter 3`, *Starting with Machine Learning*, but it is an algorithm that allows us to solve problems of supervised classification. In fact, to estimate the dependent variable, now we make use of the so-called logistic function or sigmoid. It is precisely because of this feature we call this algorithm logistic regression. The sigmoid function has the following pattern:

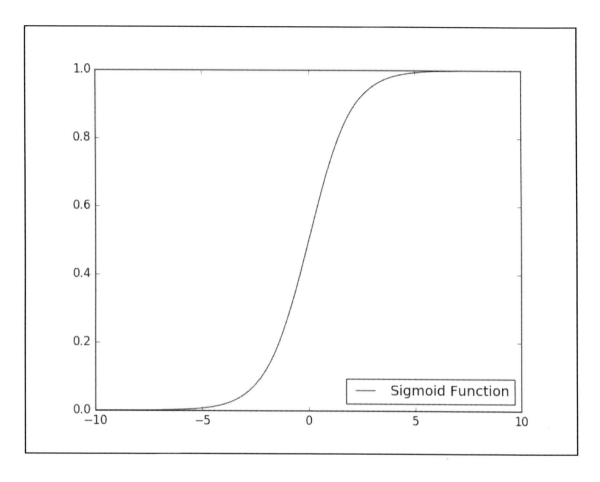

Sigmoid function

As we can see, the dependent variable takes values strictly between and 1 that is precisely what serves us. In the case of *logistic regression*, we want our function to tell us what's the *probability* of belonging to a particular element of our class. We recall again that the *supervised* learning by the neural network is configured as an *iterative process of optimization of the weights*; these are then modified on the basis of the network's performance of the training set. Indeed the aim is to minimize the *loss function*, which indicates the degree to which the behavior of the network deviates from the desired one. The performance of the network is then verified on a *test set*, consisting of images other than those of trained.

The basic steps of training that we're going to implement are as follows:

- The weights are initialized with random values at the beginning of the training.
- For each element of the training set the *error* is calculated, that is, the difference between the desired output and the actual output. This error is used to adjust the weights.
- The process is repeated, resubmitting to the network, in a random order, all the examples of the training set until the error made on the entire training set is not less than a certain threshold, or until the maximum number of iterations is reached.

Let us now see in detail how to implement the logistic regression with TensorFlow. The problem we want to solve is to classify images from the MNIST dataset, which as explained in the Chapter 3, *Starting with Machine Learning* is a database of handwritten numbers.

# TensorFlow implementation

To implementTensorFlow, we need to perform the following steps:

1. First of all, we have to import all the necessary libraries:

```
import input_data
import tensorflow as tf
import matplotlib.pyplot as plt
```

2. We use the input_data.read function introduced in Chapter 3, *Starting with Machine Learning*, in the *MNIST dataset* section, to upload the images to our problem:

```
mnist = input_data.read_data_sets("/tmp/data/", one_hot=True)
```

3. Then we set the total number of epochs for the training phase:

```
training_epochs = 25
```

4. We must also define other parameters that are necessary to build a model:

```
learning_rate = 0.01
batch_size = 100
display_step = 1
```

5. Now we move to the construction of the model.

# Building the model

Define x as the input tensor; it represents the MNIST data image of size $28 \times 28 = 784$ pixels:

```
x = tf.placeholder("float", [None, 784])
```

We recall that our problem consists of assigning a probability value for each of the possible classes of membership (the numbers from 0 to 9). At the end of this calculation, we will use a probability distribution, which gives us the value of what is confident with our prediction.

So the output we're going to get will be an output tensor with 10 probabilities, each one corresponding to a digit (of course the sum of probabilities must be one):

```
y = tf.placeholder("float", [None, 10])
```

To assign probabilities to each image, we will use the so-called softmax activation function.

The softmax function is specified in two main steps:

- Calculate the *evidence* that a certain image belongs to a particular class
- Convert the evidence into *probabilities* of belonging to each of the 10 possible classes

To evaluate the evidence, we first define the weights input tensor as W:

```
W = tf.Variable(tf.zeros([784, 10]))
```

For a given image, we can evaluate the evidence for each class i by simply multiplying the tensor W with the input tensor x. Using TensorFlow, we should have something like the following:

```
evidence = tf.matmul(x, W)
```

In general, the models include an extra parameter representing the bias, which indicates a certain degree of uncertainty. In our case, the final formula for the evidence is as follows:

```
evidence = tf.matmul(x, W) + b
```

It means that for every i (from 0 to 9) we have a Wi matrix elements $784$ $(28 \times 28)$, where each element j of the matrix is multiplied by the corresponding component j of the input image (784 parts) is added and the corresponding bias element bi.

So to define the evidence, we must define the following tensor of biases:

```
b = tf.Variable(tf.zeros([10]))
```

The second step is to finally use the `softmax` function to obtain the output vector of probabilities, namely `activation`:

```
activation = tf.nn.softmax(tf.matmul(x, W) + b)
```

TensorFlow's `tf.nn.softmax` function provides a probability-based output from the input evidence tensor. Once we implement the model, we can specify the necessary code to find the weights `W` and biases `b` network through the iterative training algorithm. In each iteration, the training algorithm takes the training data, applies the neural network, and compares the result with the expected.

 TensorFlow provides many other activation functions. See `https://www.tensorflow.org/versions/r0.8/api_docs/index.html` for better references.

In order to train our model and know when we have a good one, we must define how to define the accuracy of our model. Our goal is to try to get values of parameters `W` and `b` that minimize the value of the metric that indicates how bad the model is.

Different metrics calculated degree of error between the desired output and the training data outputs. A common measure of error is the mean squared error or the *Squared Euclidean Distance*. However, there are some research findings that suggest to use other metrics to a neural network like this.

In this example, we use the so-called `cross-entropy error` function. It is defined as:

```
cross_entropy = y*tf.lg(activation)
```

In order to minimize `cross_entropy`, we can use the following combination of `tf.reduce_mean` and `tf.reduce_sum` to build the cost function:

```
cost = tf.reduce_mean\
        (-tf.reduce_sum\
          (cross_entropy, reduction_indices=1))
```

Then we must minimize it using the gradient descent optimization algorithm:

```
optimizer = tf.train.GradientDescentOptimizer\
                (learning_rate).minimize(cost)
```

Few lines of code to build a neural net model!

# Launch the session

It's time to build the session and launch our neural net model.

We fix the following lists to visualize the training session:

```
avg_set = []
epoch_set=[]
```

Then we initialize the TensorFlow variables:

```
init = tf.initialize_all_variables()
```

Start the session:

```
with tf.Session() as sess:
    sess.run(init)
```

As explained, each epoch is a training cycle:

```
for epoch in range(training_epochs):
    avg_cost = 0.
    total_batch = int(mnist.train.num_examples/batch_size)
```

Then we loop over all the batches:

```
for i in range(total_batch):
    batch_xs, batch_ys = \
                mnist.train.next_batch(batch_size)
```

Fit the training using the batch data:

```
sess.run(optimizer, feed_dict={x: batch_xs, y: batch_ys})
```

Compute the average loss running the `train_step` function with the given image values (x) and the real output (y_):

```
avg_cost += sess.run\
            (cost, feed_dict={x: batch_xs,\
                    y: batch_ys})/total_batch
```

During computation, we display a log per epoch step:

```
if epoch % display_step == 0:
    print "Epoch:",\
            '%04d' % (epoch+1),\
            "cost=","{:.9f}".format(avg_cost)
print " Training phase finished"
```

Let's get the accuracy of our mode. It is correct if the index with the highest y value is the same as in the real digit vector the mean of the `correct_prediction` gives us the accuracy. We need to run the accuracy function with our test set (`mnist.test`).

We use the key images and labels for x and y:

```
correct_prediction = tf.equal\
                        (tf.argmax(activation, 1),\
                        tf.argmax(y, 1))
accuracy = tf.reduce_mean\
                    (tf.cast(correct_prediction, "float"))
print "MODEL accuracy:", accuracy.eval({x: mnist.test.images,\
                        y: mnist.test.labels})
```

# Test evaluation

We previously showed the training phase and for each epoch we have printed the relative cost function:

```
Python 2.7.10 (default, Oct 14 2015, 16:09:02)  [GCC 5.2.1 20151010] on
linux2 Type "copyright", "credits" or "license()" for more information. >>>
======================= RESTART ============================
>>>
Extracting /tmp/data/train-images-idx3-ubyte.gz
Extracting /tmp/data/train-labels-idx1-ubyte.gz
Extracting /tmp/data/t10k-images-idx3-ubyte.gz
Extracting /tmp/data/t10k-labels-idx1-ubyte.gz
Epoch: 0001 cost= 1.174406662
Epoch: 0002 cost= 0.661956009
Epoch: 0003 cost= 0.550468774
Epoch: 0004 cost= 0.496588717
Epoch: 0005 cost= 0.463674555
Epoch: 0006 cost= 0.440907706
Epoch: 0007 cost= 0.423837747
Epoch: 0008 cost= 0.410590841
Epoch: 0009 cost= 0.399881751
Epoch: 0010 cost= 0.390916621
Epoch: 0011 cost= 0.383320325
Epoch: 0012 cost= 0.376767031
Epoch: 0013 cost= 0.371007620
Epoch: 0014 cost= 0.365922904
Epoch: 0015 cost= 0.361327561
Epoch: 0016 cost= 0.357258660
Epoch: 0017 cost= 0.353508228
Epoch: 0018 cost= 0.350164634
Epoch: 0019 cost= 0.347015593
```

```
Epoch: 0020 cost= 0.344140861
Epoch: 0021 cost= 0.341420144
Epoch: 0022 cost= 0.338980592
Epoch: 0023 cost= 0.336655581
Epoch: 0024 cost= 0.334488012
Epoch: 0025 cost= 0.332488823
Training phase finished
```

As you can see, during the training phase the cost function is minimized. At the end of the test, we show how accurate the implemented model is:

```
Model Accuracy: 0.9475
>>>
```

Finally, using the following lines of code, we can visualize the training phase of the net:

```
plt.plot(epoch_set,avg_set, 'o',\
      label='Logistic Regression Training phase')
plt.ylabel('cost')
plt.xlabel('epoch')
plt.legend()
plt.show()
```

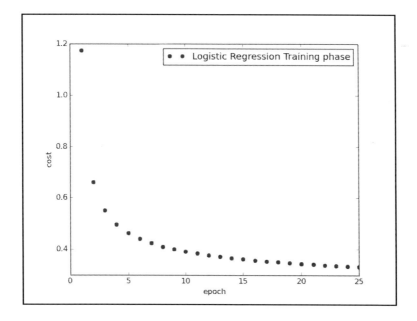

Training phase in logistic regression

# Source code

```python
# Import MINST data
import input_data
mnist = input_data.read_data_sets("/tmp/data/", one_hot=True)
import tensorflow as tf
import matplotlib.pyplot as plt
# Parameters
learning_rate = 0.01
training_epochs = 25
batch_size = 100
display_step = 1
# tf Graph Input
x = tf.placeholder("float", [None, 784])
y = tf.placeholder("float", [None, 10])
# Create model
# Set model weights
W = tf.Variable(tf.zeros([784, 10]))
b = tf.Variable(tf.zeros([10]))
# Construct model
activation = tf.nn.softmax(tf.matmul(x, W) + b)
# Minimize error using cross entropy
cross_entropy = y*tf.log(activation)
cost = tf.reduce_mean\
        (-tf.reduce_sum\
        (cross_entropy,reduction_indices=1))
optimizer = tf.train.\
            GradientDescentOptimizer(learning_rate).minimize(cost)
#Plot settings
avg_set = []
epoch_set=[]
# Initializing the variables
init = tf.initialize_all_variables()
# Launch the graph
with tf.Session() as sess:
    sess.run(init)
    # Training cycle
    for epoch in range(training_epochs):
        avg_cost = 0.
        total_batch = int(mnist.train.num_examples/batch_size)
        # Loop over all batches
        for i in range(total_batch):
            batch_xs, batch_ys = \
                    mnist.train.next_batch(batch_size)
            # Fit training using batch data
            sess.run(optimizer, \
                    feed_dict={x: batch_xs, y: batch_ys})
            # Compute average loss
```

```
        avg_cost += sess.run(cost,feed_dict=\
                                {x: batch_xs,\
                                 y: batch_ys})/total_batch
    # Display logs per epoch step
    if epoch % display_step == 0:
        print "Epoch:", '%04d' % (epoch+1),\
            "cost=", "{:.9f}".format(avg_cost)
    avg_set.append(avg_cost)
    epoch_set.append(epoch+1)
print "Training phase finished"
plt.plot(epoch_set,avg_set, 'o',\
        label='Logistic Regression Training phase')
plt.ylabel('cost')
plt.xlabel('epoch')
plt.legend()
plt.show()
# Test model
correct_prediction = tf.equal\
                    (tf.argmax(activation, 1),\
                     tf.argmax(y, 1))
# Calculate accuracy
accuracy = tf.reduce_mean(tf.cast(correct_prediction, "float"))
print "Model accuracy:", accuracy.eval({x: mnist.test.images,\
                                    y: mnist.test.labels})
```

# Multi Layer Perceptron

A more complex and efficient architecture is that of **Multi Layer Perceptron** (**MLP**). It is substantially formed from multiple layers of perceptrons, and therefore by the presence of at least *one hidden layer*, that is **not connected** either to the inputs or to the outputs of the network:

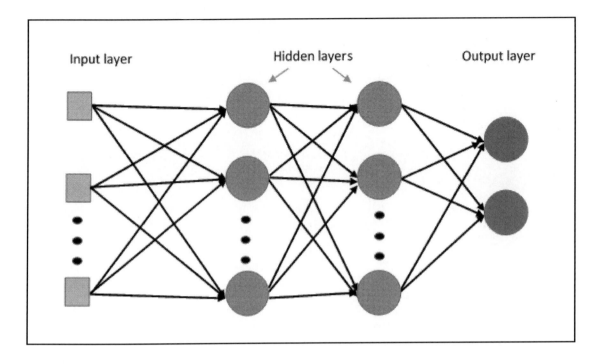

The MLP architecture

A network of this type is typically trained using supervised learning, according to the principles outlined in the previous paragraph. In particular, a typical learning algorithm for MLP networks is the so-called back propagation's algorithm.

> The back propagation algorithm is a learning algorithm for neural networks. It compares the output value of the system with the desired value. On the basis of the difference thus calculated (namely, the error), the algorithm modifies the synaptic weights of the neural network, by progressively converging the set of output values of the desired ones.

It is important to note that in MLP networks, although you don't know the desired outputs of the neurons of the hidden layers of the network, it is always possible to apply a supervised learning method based on the minimization of an error function via the application of gradient-descent techniques.

In the following example, we show the implementation with MLP for an image classification problem (MNIST).

# Multi Layer Perceptron classification

Import the necessary libraries:

```
import input_data
import tensorflow as tf
import matplotlib.pyplot as plt
```

Load the images to classify:

```
mnist = input_data.read_data_sets("/tmp/data/", one_hot=True)
```

Fix some parameters for the MLP model:

Learning rate of the net:

```
learning_rate = 0.001
```

The epochs:

```
training_epochs = 20
```

The number of images to classify:

```
batch_size = 100
display_step = 1
```

The number of neurons for the first layer:

```
n_hidden_1 = 256
```

The number of neurons for the second layer:

```
n_hidden_2 = 256
```

The size of the input (each image has 784 pixels):

```
n_input = 784 # MNIST data input (img shape: 28*28)
```

The size of of the output classes:

```
n_classes = 10
```

It should therefore be noted that while for a given application, the input and output size is perfectly defined, there are no strict criteria for how to define the number of hidden layers and the number of neurons for each layer.

Every choice must be based on experience of similar applications, as in our case:

- When increasing the number of hidden layers, we should also increase the size of the training set that is necessary and also increase the number of connections to be updated, during the learning phase. This results in an *increase* in the training time.
- Also, if there are too many neurons in the hidden layer, not only are there more weights to be updated but the network also has a tendency to learn too much from the training examples set, resulting in a *poor generalization* ability. But then if the hidden neurons are too few, the network *is not able to learn* even with the training set.

# Build the model

The input layer is the x tensor [1×784], which represents the image to classify:

```
x = tf.placeholder("float", [None, n_input])
```

The output tensor y is equal to the number of classes:

```
y = tf.placeholder("float", [None, n_classes])
```

In the middle, we have two hidden layers. The first layer is constituted by the h tensor of weights, whose size is [784 × 256], where 256 is the total number of nodes of the layer:

```
h = tf.Variable(tf.random_normal([n_input, n_hidden_1]))
```

For layer 1, so we have to define the respective biases tensor:

```
bias_layer_1 = tf.Variable(tf.random_normal([n_hidden_1]))
```

Each neuron receives the pixels of input image to be classified combined with the hij weight connections and added to the respective values of the biases tensor:

```
layer_1 = tf.nn.sigmoid(tf.add(tf.matmul(x,h),bias_layer_1))
```

It sends its output to the neurons of the next layer through the `activation` function. It must be said that functions can be different from one neuron to another, but in practice, however, we adopt a common feature for all the neurons, typically of the sigmoidal type. Sometimes the output neurons are equipped with a linear activation function. It is interesting to note that the activation functions of the neurons in the hidden layers cannot be linear because, in this case, the MLP network would be equivalent to a network with two layers and therefore no longer of the MLP type. The second layer must perform *the same steps as the first.*

The second intermediate layer is represented by the shape of the weights tensor `[256 × 256]`:

```
w = tf.Variable(tf.random_normal([n_hidden_1, n_hidden_2]))
```

With the tensor of biases:

```
bias_layer_2 = tf.Variable(tf.random_normal([n_hidden_2]))
```

Each neuron in this second layer receives inputs from the neurons of layer 1, combined with the weight `Wij` connections and added to the respective biases of layer 2:

```
layer_2 = tf.nn.sigmoid(tf.add(tf.matmul(layer_1,w),bias_layer_2))
```

It sends its output to the next layer, namely the output layer:

```
output = tf.Variable(tf.random_normal([n_hidden_2, n_classes]))
bias_output = tf.Variable(tf.random_normal([n_classes]))
output_layer = tf.matmul(layer_2, output) + bias_output
```

The output layer receives as input n-stimuli (256) coming from layer 2, which is converted to the respective classes of probability for each number.

As for the logistic regression, we then define the `cost` function:

```
cost = tf.reduce_mean\
    (tf.nn.softmax_cross_entropy_with_logits\
(output_layer, y))
```

The TensorFlow function `tf.nn.softmax_cross_entropy_with_logits` computes the cost for a softmax layer. It is only used during training. The logits are the unnormalized log probabilities output the model (the values output before the softmax normalization is applied to them).

The corresponding optimizer that minimizes the `cost` function is:

```
optimizer = tf.train.AdamOptimizer\
        (learning_rate=learning_rate).minimize(cost)
```

`tf.train.AdamOptimizer` uses Kingma and Ba's Adam algorithm to control the learning rate. Adam offers several advantages over the simple `tf.train.GradientDescentOptimizer`. In fact, it uses a larger effective step size, and the algorithm will converge to this step size without fine tuning.

A simple `tf.train.GradientDescentOptimizer` could equally be used in your MLP, but would require more hyper parameter tuning before it could converge as quickly.

 TensorFlow provides the optimizer base class to compute gradients for a loss and apply gradients to variables. This class defines the API to add ops to train a model. You never use this class directly, but instead instantiate one of its sub classes. See `https://www.tensorflow.org/versions/r0.8/api_docs/python/train.html#Optimizer` to see the optimizer implemented.

# Launch the session

The following are the steps to launch the session:

1. Plot the settings:

```
avg_set = []
epoch_set=[]
```

2. Initialize the variables:

```
init = tf.initialize_all_variables()
```

3. Launch the graph:

```
with tf.Session() as sess:
    sess.run(init)
```

4. Define the training cycle:

```
for epoch in range(training_epochs):
    avg_cost = 0.
    total_batch = int(mnist.train.num_examples/batch_size)
```

5. Loop over all the batches (100):

```
for i in range(total_batch):
    batch_xs, batch_ys = mnist.train.next_batch(batch_size)
```

6. Fit training using the batch data:

```
sess.run(optimizer, feed_dict={x: batch_xs, y: batch_ys})
```

7. Compute the average loss:

```
avg_cost += sess.run(cost,feed_dict={x: batch_xs,\
        y: batch_ys})/total_batch
Display logs per epoch step
if epoch % display_step == 0:
    print "Epoch:", '%04d' % (epoch+1),\
    "cost=", "{:.9f}".format(avg_cost)
avg_set.append(avg_cost)
epoch_set.append(epoch+1)
print "Training phase finished"
```

8. With these lines of codes, we plot the training phase:

```
plt.plot(epoch_set,avg_set, 'o', label='MLP Training phase')
plt.ylabel('cost')
plt.xlabel('epoch')
plt.legend()
plt.show()
```

9. Finally, we can test the MLP model:

```
correct_prediction = tf.equal(tf.argmax(output_layer, 1),\
        tf.argmax(y, 1))
evaluating its accuracy
accuracy = tf.reduce_mean(tf.cast(correct_prediction, "float"))
print "Model Accuracy:", accuracy.eval({x: mnist.test.images,\
            y: mnist.test.labels})
```

10. Here is the output result after 20 epochs:

```
Python 2.7.10 (default, Oct 14 2015, 16:09:02)  [GCC 5.2.1 20151010] on
linux2 Type "copyright", "credits" or "license()" for more information.
>>> ========================== RESTART ==============================
>>>
Succesfully downloaded train-images-idx3-ubyte.gz 9912422 bytes.
Extracting /tmp/data/train-images-idx3-ubyte.gz
Succesfully downloaded train-labels-idx1-ubyte.gz 28881 bytes.
Extracting /tmp/data/train-labels-idx1-ubyte.gz
Succesfully downloaded t10k-images-idx3-ubyte.gz 1648877 bytes.
Extracting /tmp/data/t10k-images-idx3-ubyte.gz
Succesfully downloaded t10k-labels-idx1-ubyte.gz 4542 bytes.
Extracting /tmp/data/t10k-labels-idx1-ubyte.gz
Epoch: 0001 cost= 1.723947845
Epoch: 0002 cost= 0.539266024
Epoch: 0003 cost= 0.362600502
Epoch: 0004 cost= 0.266637279
Epoch: 0005 cost= 0.205345784
Epoch: 0006 cost= 0.159139332
Epoch: 0007 cost= 0.125232637
Epoch: 0008 cost= 0.098572041
Epoch: 0009 cost= 0.077509963
Epoch: 0010 cost= 0.061127526
Epoch: 0011 cost= 0.048033808
Epoch: 0012 cost= 0.037297983
Epoch: 0013 cost= 0.028884999
Epoch: 0014 cost= 0.022818390
Epoch: 0015 cost= 0.017447586
Epoch: 0016 cost= 0.013652348
Epoch: 0017 cost= 0.010417282
Epoch: 0018 cost= 0.008079228
Epoch: 0019 cost= 0.006203546
Epoch: 0020 cost= 0.004961207
Training phase finished
Model Accuracy: 0.9775
>>>
```

We show the training phase in the following figure:

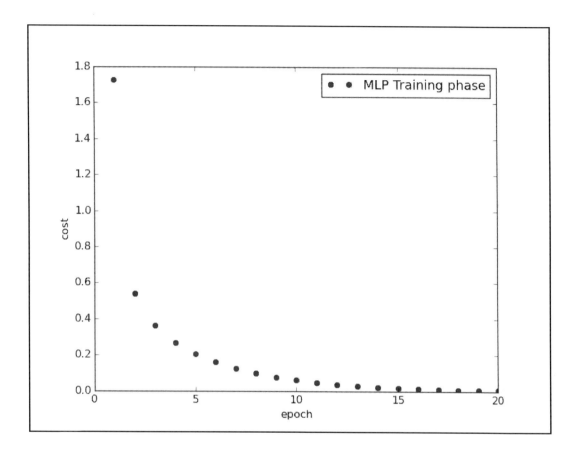

Training phase in Multi Layer Perceptron

# Source code

```
# Import MINST data
import input_data
mnist = input_data.read_data_sets("/tmp/data/", one_hot=True)
import tensorflow as tf
import matplotlib.pyplot as plt
# Parameters
learning_rate = 0.001
training_epochs = 20
batch_size = 100
display_step = 1
```

```
# Network Parameters
n_hidden_1 = 256 # 1st layer num features
n_hidden_2 = 256 # 2nd layer num features
n_input = 784 # MNIST data input (img shape: 28*28)
n_classes = 10 # MNIST total classes (0-9 digits)
# tf Graph input
x = tf.placeholder("float", [None, n_input])
y = tf.placeholder("float", [None, n_classes])
#weights layer 1
h = tf.Variable(tf.random_normal([n_input, n_hidden_1]))
#bias layer 1
bias_layer_1 = tf.Variable(tf.random_normal([n_hidden_1]))
#layer 1
layer_1 = tf.nn.sigmoid(tf.add(tf.matmul(x,h),bias_layer_1))
#weights layer 2
w = tf.Variable(tf.random_normal([n_hidden_1, n_hidden_2]))
#bias layer 2
bias_layer_2 = tf.Variable(tf.random_normal([n_hidden_2]))
#layer 2
layer_2 = tf.nn.sigmoid(tf.add(tf.matmul(layer_1,w),bias_layer_2))
#weights output layer
output = tf.Variable(tf.random_normal([n_hidden_2, n_classes]))
#biar output layer
bias_output = tf.Variable(tf.random_normal([n_classes]))
#output layer
output_layer = tf.matmul(layer_2, output) + bias_output
# cost function
cost = tf.reduce_mean\
    (tf.nn.softmax_cross_entropy_with_logits(output_layer, y))
# optimizer
optimizer = tf.train.AdamOptimizer\
      (learning_rate=learning_rate).minimize(cost)
#Plot settings
avg_set = []
epoch_set=[]
# Initializing the variables
init = tf.initialize_all_variables()
# Launch the graph
with tf.Session() as sess:
    sess.run(init)
    # Training cycle
    for epoch in range(training_epochs):
        avg_cost = 0.
        total_batch = int(mnist.train.num_examples/batch_size)
        # Loop over all batches
        for i in range(total_batch):
            batch_xs, batch_ys = mnist.train.next_batch(batch_size)
            # Fit training using batch data
```

```
            sess.run(optimizer, feed_dict={x: batch_xs, y: batch_ys})
            # Compute average loss
            avg_cost += sess.run(cost, \
        feed_dict={x: batch_xs,\
            y: batch_ys})/total_batch
        # Display logs per epoch step
        if epoch % display_step == 0:
            print "Epoch:", '%04d' % (epoch+1),\
          "cost=", "{:.9f}".format(avg_cost)
        avg_set.append(avg_cost)
        epoch_set.append(epoch+1)
    print "Training phase finished"
    plt.plot(epoch_set,avg_set, 'o', label='MLP Training phase')
    plt.ylabel('cost')
    plt.xlabel('epoch')
    plt.legend()
    plt.show()
    # Test model
    correct_prediction = tf.equal(tf.argmax(output_layer, 1),\
        tf.argmax(y, 1))
    # Calculate accuracy
    accuracy = tf.reduce_mean(tf.cast(correct_prediction, "float"))
    print "Model Accuracy:", accuracy.eval({x: mnist.test.images,\
y: mnist.test.labels})
```

# Multi Layer Perceptron function approximation

In the following example, we implement an MLP network that will be able to learn the trend of an arbitrary function $f(x)$. In the training phase the network will have to learn from a known set of points, that is $x$ and $f(x)$, while in the test phase the network will deduct the values of $f(x)$ only from the $x$ values.

This very simple network will be built by a single hidden layer.

Import the necessary libraries:

```
import tensorflow as tf
import numpy as np
import math, random
import matplotlib.pyplot as plt
```

We build the data model. The function to be learned will follow the trend of the `cosine` function, evaluated for 1000 points to which we add a very little random error (noise) to reproduce a real case:

```
NUM_points = 1000
np.random.seed(NUM_points)
function_to_learn = lambda x: np.cos(x) + \
        0.1*np.random.randn(*x.shape)
```

Our MLP network will be formed by a hidden layer of 10 neurons:

```
layer_1_neurons = 10
```

The network learns for 100 points at a time to a total of 1500 learning cycles (epochs):

```
batch_size = 100
NUM_EPOCHS = 1500
```

Finally, we construct the training set and the test set:

```
all_x contiene tutti i punti
all_x = np.float32(np.random.uniform\
    (-2*math.pi, 2*math.pi,\
        (1, NUM_points))).T
np.random.shuffle(all_x)
train_size = int(900)
```

The first 900 points are in the training set:

```
x_training = all_x[:train_size]
y_training = function_to_learn(x_training)
```

The last 100 will be in the validation set:

```
x_validation = all_x[train_size:]
y_validation = function_to_learn(x_validation)
```

Using matplotlib, we display these sets:

```
plt.figure(1)
plt.scatter(x_training, y_training, c='blue', label='train')
plt.scatter(x_validation, y_validation,c='red',label='validation')
plt.legend()
plt.show()
```

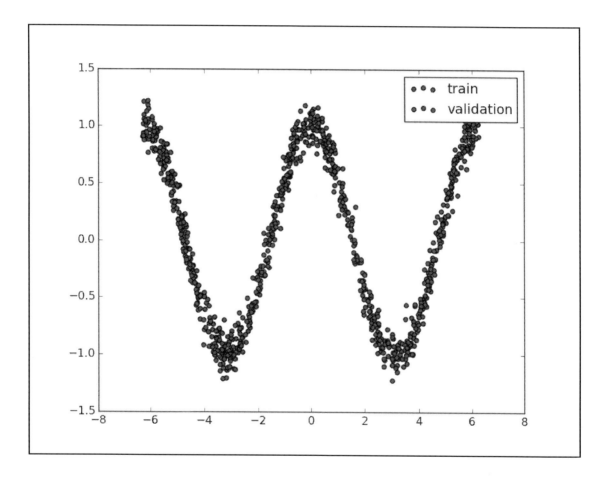

Training and validation set

# Build the model

First, we create the placeholders for the input tensor (X) and the output tensor (Y):

```
X = tf.placeholder(tf.float32, [None, 1], name="X")
Y = tf.placeholder(tf.float32, [None, 1], name="Y")
```

Then we build the hidden layer of [1 x 10] dimensions:

```
w_h = tf.Variable(tf.random_uniform([1, layer_1_neurons],\
                                     minval=-1, maxval=1, \
dtype=tf.float32))
  b_h = tf.Variable(tf.zeros([1, layer_1_neurons], \
                             dtype=tf.float32))
```

It receives the input value from the X input tensor, combined with the weight w_hij connections and added with the respective biases of layer 1:

```
h = tf.nn.sigmoid(tf.matmul(X, w_h) + b_h)
```

The output layer is a [10 x 1] tensor:

```
w_o = tf.Variable(tf.random_uniform([layer_1_neurons, 1],\
                              minval=-1, maxval=1,\
                              dtype=tf.float32))
    b_o = tf.Variable(tf.zeros([1, 1], dtype=tf.float32))
```

Each neuron in this second layer receives inputs from the neurons of layer 1, combined with weight w_oij connections and added together with the respective biases of the output layer:

```
model = tf.matmul(h, w_o) + b_o
```

We then define our optimizer for the newly defined model:

```
train_op = tf.train.AdamOptimizer().minimize\
        (tf.nn.l2_loss(model - Y))
```

We also note that in this case, the cost function adopted is the following:

```
tf.nn.l2_loss(model - Y)
```

The tf.nn.l2_loss function is a TensorFlow that computes half the L2 norm of a tensor without the sqrt, that is, the output for the preceding function is as follows:

```
output = sum((model - Y) ** 2) / 2
```

The tf.nn.l2_loss function can be a viable cost function for our example.

# Launch the session

Let's build the evaluation graph:

```
sess = tf.Session()
sess.run(tf.initialize_all_variables())
```

Now we can launch the learning session:

```
errors = []
for i in range(NUM_EPOCHS):
    for start, end in zip(range(0, len(x_training), batch_size),\
                          range(batch_size,\
                                len(x_training), batch_size)):
        sess.run(train_op, feed_dict={X: x_training[start:end],\
                                      Y: y_training[start:end]})
    cost = sess.run(tf.nn.l2_loss(model - y_validation),\
                    feed_dict={X:x_validation})
    errors.append(cost)
    if i%100 == 0: print "epoch %d, cost = %g" % (i, cost)
```

Running this network for 1400 epochs, we'll see the error progressively reducing and eventually converging:

```
Python 2.7.10 (default, Oct 14 2015, 16:09:02)  [GCC 5.2.1 20151010] on
linux2 Type "copyright", "credits" or "license()" for more information.
>>> ====================== RESTART =============================
>>>
epoch 0, cost = 55.9286
epoch 100, cost = 22.0084
epoch 200, cost = 18.033
epoch 300, cost = 14.0481
epoch 400, cost = 9.74721
epoch 500, cost = 5.83419
epoch 600, cost = 3.05434
epoch 700, cost = 1.53706
epoch 800, cost = 0.91719
epoch 900, cost = 0.726675
epoch 1000, cost = 0.668316
epoch 1100, cost = 0.633737
epoch 1200, cost = 0.608306
epoch 1300, cost = 0.590429
epoch 1400, cost = 0.574602
>>>
```

The following lines of code allow us to display how the cost changes in the running epochs:

```
plt.plot(errors,label='MLP Function Approximation')
plt.xlabel('epochs')
plt.ylabel('cost')
plt.legend()
plt.show()
```

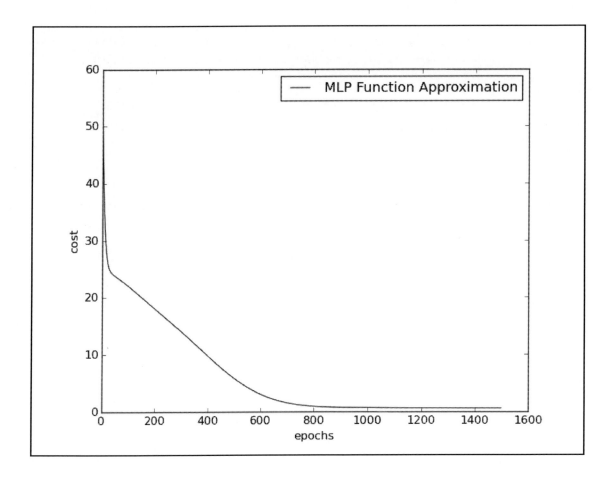

Training phase in Multi Layer Perceptron

# Summary

In this chapter, we introduced *artificial neural networks*. An artificial neuron is a mathematical model that to some extent mimics the properties of a living neurons. Each neuron of the network has a very simple operation which consists of becoming active if the total amount of signal that it receives exceeds a look at the activation threshold. The learning process is typically *supervised*: the neural net uses a training set to infer the relationship between the input and the corresponding output, while the learning algorithm modifies the weights of the net in order to *minimize a cost function* that represents the *forecast error* relating to the *training set*. If the training is successful, the neural net will be able to make forecasts even where the output is not known a priori. In this chapter we implemented, using TensorFlow, some examples involving neural networks. We have seen neural nets used to solve classification and regressions problems as the *logistic regression* algorithm in a classification problem using the *Rosemblatt's Perceptron*. At the end of the chapter, we introduced the *Multi Layer Perceptron* architecture, which we have seen in action prior to the implementation of an *image classifier*, then for a *simulator of mathematical functions*.

In the next chapter, we finally introduce deep learning models; we will examine and implement more complex neural network architectures, such as a convolutional neural network and a recurrent neural network.

# 5
# Deep Learning

In this chapter, we will cover the following topics:

- Deep learning techniques
- Convolutional neural network (CNN)
    - CNN architecture
    - TensorFlow implementation of a CNN
- Recurrent neural network (RNN)
    - RNN architecture
    - Natural Language Processing with TensorFlow

## Deep learning techniques

Deep learning techniques are a crucial step forward taken by the machine learning researchers in recent decades, having provided successful results ever seen before in many applications, such as image recognition and speech recognition.

There are several reasons that led to deep learning being developed and placed at the center of attention in the scope of machine learning. One of these reasons is represented by the progress in hardware, with the availability of new processors, such as graphics processing units (**GPUs**), which have greatly reduced the time needed for training networks, lowering them 10/20 times.

Another reason is certainly the increasing ease of *finding* ever more numerous *datasets* on which to train a system, needed to train architectures of a certain depth and with high dimensionality of the input data. Deep learning consists of a set of methods that allow a system to obtain a *hierarchical representation* of the data on multiple levels. This is achieved by combining simple units (not linear), each of which transforms the representation at its own level, starting from the input level, to a representation at a higher, level slightly *more abstract*. With a sufficient number of these transformations, considerably complex input-output functions can be learned.

With reference to a classification problem, for example, the highest levels of representation, highlight the aspects of the input data that are relevant for the classification, suppressing the ones that have no effect on the classification purposes.

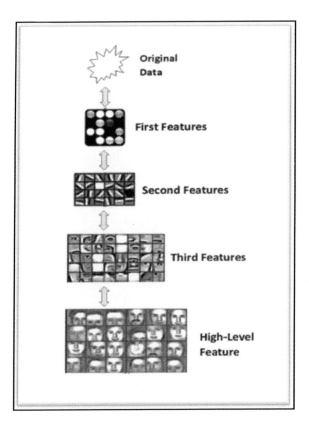

Hierarchical feature extraction in an image classification system

The preceding scheme describes the features of the image classification system (a face recognizer): each block gradually extracts the features of the input image, going to process data already pre-processed from the previous blocks, extracting increasingly complex features of the input image, and thus building the hierarchical data representation that characterizes a deep learning-based system.

A possible representation of the features of the hierarchy could be as follows:

```
pixel --> edge --> texture --> motif --> part --> object
```

In a text recognition problem, however, the hierarchical representation can be structured as follows:

```
character --> word --> word group --> clause --> sentence --> story
```

A deep learning architecture is, therefore, a *multi-level architecture*, consisting of simple units, all subject to training, many of which carry *non-linear transformations*. Each unit transforms its input to improve its *properties to select and amplify* only the relevant aspects for classification purposes, and its *invariance*, namely its propensity *to ignore* the irrelevant aspects and negligible.

With multiple levels of non-linear transformations, therefore, with a depth approximately between 5 and 20 levels, a deep learning system can learn and implement extremely intricate and complex functions, simultaneously *very sensitive* to the smallest relevant details, and extremely *insensitive* and *indifferent* to large variations of irrelevant aspects of the input data which can be, in the case of object recognition: image's background, brightness, or the position of the represented object.

The following sections will illustrate, with the aid of TensorFlow, two important types of deep neural networks: the **convolutional neural networks** (**CNNs**), mainly addressed to the classification problems, and then the **recurrent neural networks** (**RNNs**), targeting **Natural Language Processing** (**NLP**) issues.

# Convolutional neural networks

**Convolutional neural networks** (**CNNs**) are a particular type of neural network-oriented deep learning that have achieved excellent results in many practical applications, in particular the *object recognition* in images.

In fact, CNNs are designed to process data represented in the form of multiple arrays, for example, the *color images*, representable by means of three two-dimensional arrays containing the pixel's color intensity. The substantial difference between CNNs and ordinary neural networks is that the former *operate directly* on the images while the latter on *features extracted* from them. The input of a CNN, therefore, unlike that of an ordinary neural network, will be *two-dimensional*, and the features will be the pixels of the input image.

The CNN is the dominant approach for almost all the problems of recognition. The spectacular performance offered by networks of this type have in fact prompted the biggest companies in technology, such as Google and Facebook, to invest in research and development projects for networks of this kind, and to develop and distribute products image recognition based on CNNs.

## CNN architecture

The CNN use three basic ideas: *local receptive fields*, *convolution*, and *pooling*.

In convolutional networks, we consider input as something similar to what is shown in the following figure:

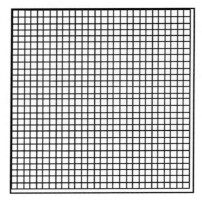

Input neurons

One of the concepts behind CNNs is *local connectivity*. CNNs, in fact, utilize spatial correlations that may exist within the input data. Each neuron of the first subsequent layer connects*only some* of the input neurons. This region is called **local receptive field**. In the following figure, it is represented by the black 5Ã5 square that *converges* to a hidden neuron:

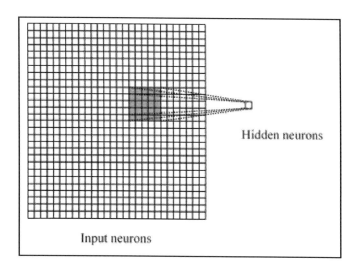

From input to hidden neurons

The *hidden neuron*, of course, will only process the input data inside of its receptive field, not realizing the changes outside of that. However, it is easy to see that, by superimposing several layers, that are locally connected, leveling up you will have units that process more and more *global data* compared to input, in accordance with the basic principle of deep learning, to bring the performance to a level of abstraction that is always growing.

The reason for the local connectivity resides in the fact that in data of arrays form, such as the images, the values are often highly correlated, forming distinct groups of data that can be easily identified.

Each connection learns a weight (so it will get 5Ã5 = 25), instead of the hidden neuron with an associated connecting learns a total bias, then we are going to connect the regions to individual neurons by performing a shift from time to time, as in the following figures:

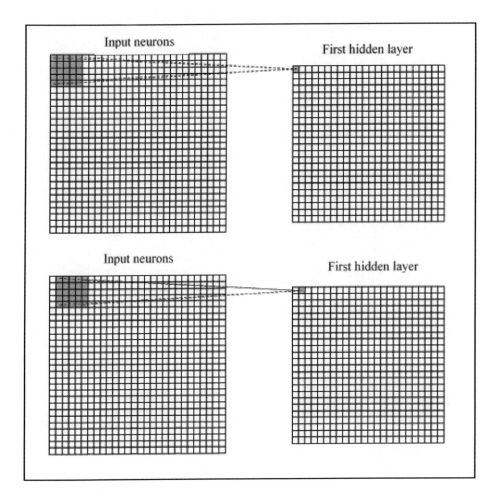

The convolution operation

This operation is called **convolution**. Doing so, if we have an image of 28Ã28 inputs and 5Ã5 regions, we will get 24Ã24 neurons in the hidden layer. We said that each neuron has a bias and 5Ã5 weights connected to the region: we will use these weights and biases for all 24Ã24 neurons. This means that all the neurons in the first hidden layer will recognize the same features, just placed differently in the input image. For this reason, the map of connections from the input layer to the hidden feature map is called *shared weights* and bias is called *shared bias*, since they are in fact shared.

Obviously, we need to recognize an image of more than a map of features, so a complete convolutional layer is made from *multiple feature maps*.

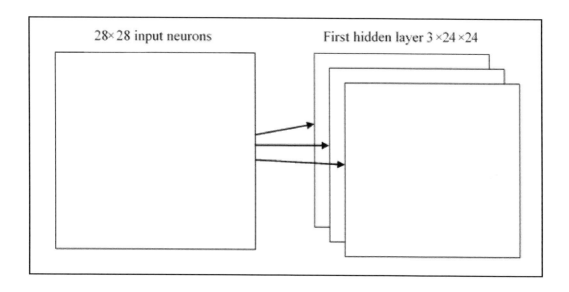

Multiple feature maps

In the preceding figure, we see three feature maps; of course, its number can increase in practice and you can get to use convolutional layers with even 20 or 40 feature maps. A great advantage in the sharing of weights and bias is the *significant reduction* of the parameters involved in a convolutional network. Considering our example, for each feature map we need 25 weights (5Ã⊙5) and a bias (shared); that is 26 parameters in total. Assuming we have 20 feature maps, we will have 520 parameters to be defined. With a fully connected network, with 784 input neurons and, for example, 30 hidden layer neurons, we need 30 more 784Ã⊙30 bias weights, reaching a total of 23.550 parameters.

The difference is evident. The convolutional networks also use *pooling layers*, which are layers immediately positioned after the convolutional layers; these simplify the output information of the previous layer to it (*the convolution*). It takes the input feature maps coming out of the convolutional layer and prepares a *condensed* feature map. For example, we can say that the pooling layer could be summed up, in all its units, in a 2Ã⊙2 region of neurons of the previous layer.

This technique is called pooling and can be summarized with the following scheme:

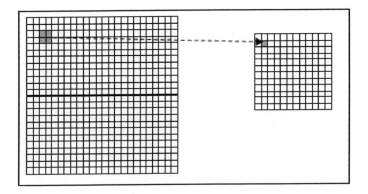

The pooling operation helps to simplify the information from a layer to the next

Obviously, we usually have more features maps and we apply the maximum pooling to each of them separately.

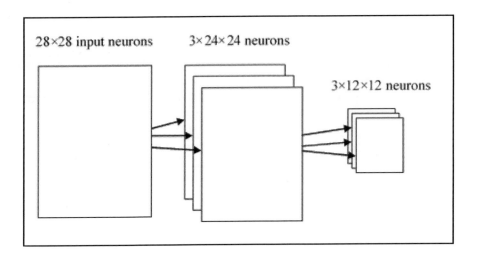

From the input layer to the second hidden layer

So we have three feature maps of size 24Ã24 for the first hidden layer, and the second hidden layer will be of size 12Ã12, since we are assuming that for every unit summarize a 2Ã2 region.

Combining these three ideas, we form a complete convolutional network. Its architecture can be displayed as follows:

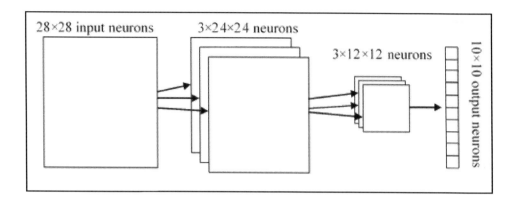

A CNNs architectural schema

Let's summarize: there are the 28Ã⊚28 input neurons followed by a *convolutional layer* with a local receptive field 5Ã⊚5 and 3 feature maps. We obtain as a result of *a hidden layer* of neurons 3Ã⊚24Ã⊚24. Then there is the max-pooling applied to 2Ã⊚2 on the 3 regions of feature maps getting a hidden layer 3Ã⊚12Ã⊚12. The last layer is *fully connected*: it connects all the neurons of the max-pooling layer to all 10 output neurons, useful to recognize the corresponding output.

This network will then be trained by gradient descent and the back propagation algorithm.

# TensorFlow implementation of a CNN

In the following example, we will see in action the CNN in a problem of image classification. We want to show the process of building a CNN network: what are the steps to execute and what reasoning needs to be done to run a proper dimensioning of the entire network, and of course how to implement it with TensorFlow.

### Initialization step

1. Load and prepare the MNIST data:

```
import tensorflow as tf
import input_data
mnist = input_data.read_data_sets("/tmp/data/", one_hot=True)
```

2. Define all the CNN parameters:

```
learning_rate = 0.001
training_iters = 100000
batch_size = 128
display_step = 10
```

3. MNIST data input (each shape is of 28Ã◉28 array pixels):

```
n_input = 784
```

4. The MNIST total classes (0-9 digits)

```
n_classes = 10
```

5. To reduce the over fitting, we apply the *dropout* technique. This term refers to dropping out units (hidden, input, and output) in a neural network. Deciding which neurons to eliminate is random; one way is to apply a probability, as we shall see in our code. For this reason, we define the following parameter (to be tuned):

```
dropout = 0.75
```

6. Define the placeholders for the input graph. The x placeholder contains the MNIST data input (exactly 728 pixels):

```
x = tf.placeholder(tf.float32, [None, n_input])
```

7. Then we change the form of 4D input images to a tensor, using the TensorFlow reshape operator:

```
_X = tf.reshape(x, shape=[-1, 28, 28, 1])
```

The second and third dimensions correspond to the width and height of the image, while the latter dimension is the total number of color channels (in our case 1).

So we can display our input image as a two-dimensional tensor, of size 28Ã©28:

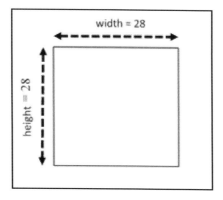

The input tensor for our problem

The output tensor will contain the *output probability* for each digit to classify:

```
y = tf.placeholder(tf.float32, [None, n_classes]).
```

## First convolutional layer

Each neuron of the hidden layer is connected to a small subset of the input tensor of dimension 5Ã©5. This implies that the hidden layer will have a 24Ã©24 size. We also define and initialize the tensors of shared weights and shared bias:

```
wc1 = tf.Variable(tf.random_normal([5, 5, 1, 32]))
bc1 = tf.Variable(tf.random_normal([32]))
```

Recall that in order to recognize an image, we need more than a map of features. The number is just the number of feature maps we are considering for this first layer. In our case, the convolutional layer is composed of 32 feature maps.

The next step is the construction of the *first convolution layer*, `conv1`:

```
conv1 = conv2d(_X,wc1,bc1)
```

Here, `conv2d` is the following function:

```
def conv2d(img, w, b):
  return tf.nn.relu(tf.nn.bias_add\
                    (tf.nn.conv2d(img, w,\
                                  strides=[1, 1, 1, 1],\
                                  padding='SAME'),b))
```

For this purpose, we used the TensorFlow `tf.nn.conv2d` function. It computes a 2D convolution from the *input tensor* and the *shared weights*. The result of this operation will be then added to the biases `bc1` matrix. For this purpose, we used the function `tf.nn.conv2d` to compute a 2-D convolution from the input tensor and the tensor of shared weights. The result of this operation will be then added to the biases `bc1` matrix. While `tf.nn.relu` is the *Relu function* (Rectified linear unit) that is the *usual activation function* in the hidden layer of a deep neural network.

We will apply this activation function to the return value that we have with the convolution function. The padding value is `'SAME'`, which indicates that *the output tensor output will have the same size of input tensor*.

One way to represent the convolutional layer, namely `conv1`, is as follows:

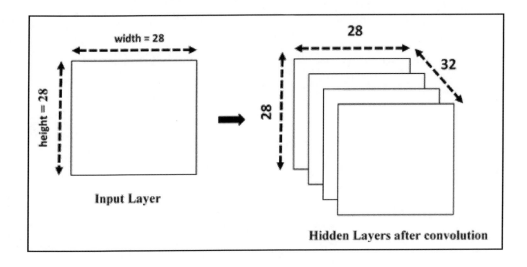

The first hidden layer

After the convolution operation, we impose the *pooling* step that simplifies the output information of the previously created convolutional layer.

In our example, let's take a 2Ã©2 region of the convolution layer and we will summarize the information at each point in the pooling layer.

```
conv1 = max_pool(conv1, k=2)
```

Here, for the pooling operation, we have implemented the following function:

```
def max_pool(img, k):
    return tf.nn.max_pool(img, \
                          ksize=[1, k, k, 1],\
                          strides=[1, k, k, 1],\
                          padding='SAME')
```

The `tf.nn.max_pool` function performs the max pooling on the input. Of course, we apply the max pooling for each convolutional layer, and there will be many layers of pooling and convolution. At the end of the pooling phase, we'll have 12Ã©12Ã©32 *convolutional hidden layers*.

The next figure shows the CNNs layers after the pooling and convolution operation:

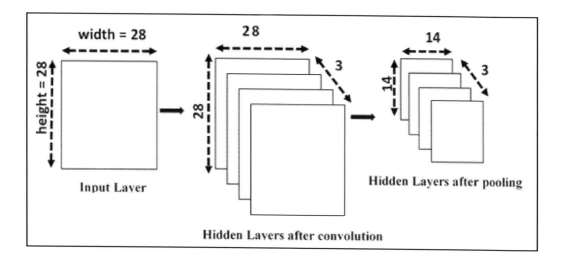

The CNNs after a first convolution and pooling operations

The last operation is to reduce the overfitting by applying the `tf.nn.dropout` TensorFlow operators on the convolutional layer. To do this, we create a placeholder for the probability (`keep_prob`) that a neuron's output is kept during the dropout:

```
keep_prob = tf. placeholder(tf.float32)
conv1 = tf.nn.dropout(conv1,keep_prob)
```

## Second convolutional layer

For the *second hidden layer*, we must apply the same operations as the first layer, and so we define and initialize the tensors of *shared weights* and *shared bias*:

```
wc2 = tf.Variable(tf.random_normal([5, 5, 32, 64]))
bc2 = tf.Variable(tf.random_normal([64]))
```

As you can note, this second hidden layer will have 64 features for a 5×5 window, while the number of input layers will be given from the first convolutional obtained layer. We next apply a second layer to the convolutional conv1 tensor, but this time we apply 64 sets of 5×5 filters each to the 32 conv1 layers:

```
conv2 = conv2d(conv1,wc2,bc2)
```

It give us 64 14×14 arrays which we reduce with max pooling to 64 7×7 arrays:

```
conv2 = max_pool(conv2, k=2)
```

Finally, we again use the dropout operation:

```
conv2 = tf.nn.dropout(conv2, keep_prob)
```

The resulting layer is a 7×7 x 64 convolution tensor because we started from the input tensor 12×12 and a sliding window of 5×5, considering that has a stride of 1.

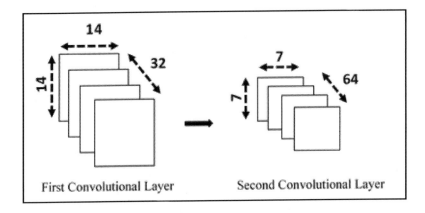

Building the second hidden layer

## Densely connected layer

In this step, we build a densely connected layer that we use to process the entire image. The weight and bias tensors are as follows:

```
wd1 = tf.Variable(tf.random_normal([7*7*64, 1024]))
bd1 = tf.Variable(tf.random_normal([1024]))
```

As you can note, this layer will be formed by 1024 neurons.

Then we reshape the tensor from the second convolutional layer into a batch of vectors:

```
dense1 = tf.reshape(conv2, [-1, wd1.get_shape().as_list()[0]])
```

Multiply this tensor by the weight matrix, wd1, add the tensor bias, bd1, and apply a RELU operation:

```
dense1 = tf.nn.relu(tf.add(tf.matmul(dense1, wd1),bd1))
```

We complete this layer by again using the dropout operator:

```
dense1 = tf.nn.dropout(dense1, keep_prob)
```

## Readout layer

The last layer defines the tensors wout and bout:

```
wout = tf.Variable(tf.random_normal([1024, n_classes]))
bout = tf.Variable(tf.random_normal([n_classes]))
```

Before applying the softmax function, we must calculate the *evidence* that the image belongs to a certain class:

```
pred = tf.add(tf.matmul(dense1, wout), bout)
```

## Testing and training the model

The evidence must be converted into probabilities for each of the 10 possible classes (the method is identical to what we saw in Chapter 4, *Introducing Neural Networks*). So we define the cost function, which evaluates the quality of our model, by applying the softmax function:

```
cost = tf.reduce_mean(tf.nn.softmax_cross_entropy_with_logits(pred, y))
```

And its function optimization, using the TensorFlow `AdamOptimizer` function:

```
optimizer =
tf.train.AdamOptimizer(learning_rate=learning_rate).minimize(cost)
```

The following tensor will serve in the evaluation phase of the model:

```
correct_pred = tf.equal(tf.argmax(pred,1), tf.argmax(y,1))
accuracy = tf.reduce_mean(tf.cast(correct_pred, tf.float32))
```

## Launching the session

Initialize the variables:

```
init = tf.initialize_all_variables()
```

Build the evaluation graph:

```
with tf.Session() as sess:
    sess.run(init)
    step = 1
```

Let's train the net until `training_iters`:

```
while step * batch_size < training_iters:
    batch_xs, batch_ys = mnist.train.next_batch(batch_size)
```

Fit training using the `batch` data:

```
sess.run(optimizer, feed_dict={x: batch_xs,\
                               y: batch_ys,\
                               keep_prob:  dropout})
    if step % display_step == 0:
```

Calculate the `accuracy`:

```
acc = sess.run(accuracy, feed_dict={x: batch_xs,\
                                    y: batch_ys,\
                                    keep_prob: 1.})
```

Calculate the `loss`:

```
loss = sess.run(cost, feed_dict={x: batch_xs,\
                                 y: batch_ys,\
                                 keep_prob: 1.})
    print "Iter " + str(step*batch_size) +\
        ", Minibatch Loss= " + \
        "{:.6f}".format(loss) + \
```

```
                ", Training Accuracy= " + \
                "{:.5f}".format(acc)
        step += 1
    print "Optimization Finished!"
```

We print the accuracy for the 256 MNIST test images:

```
print "Testing Accuracy:",\
        sess.run(accuracy,\
            feed_dict={x: mnist.test.images[:256], \
                        y: mnist.test.labels[:256],\
                        keep_prob: 1.})
```

Running the code, we have the following output:

```
Extracting /tmp/data/train-images-idx3-ubyte.gz
Extracting /tmp/data/train-labels-idx1-ubyte.gz
Extracting /tmp/data/t10k-images-idx3-ubyte.gz
Extracting /tmp/data/t10k-labels-idx1-ubyte.gz
Iter 1280, Minibatch Loss= 27900.769531,
Training Accuracy= 0.17188
Iter 2560, Minibatch Loss= 17168.949219, Training Accuracy= 0.21094
Iter 3840, Minibatch Loss= 15000.724609, Training Accuracy= 0.41406
Iter 5120, Minibatch Loss= 8000.896484, Training Accuracy= 0.49219
Iter 6400, Minibatch Loss= 4587.275391, Training Accuracy= 0.61719
Iter 7680, Minibatch Loss= 5949.988281, Training Accuracy= 0.69531
Iter 8960, Minibatch Loss= 4932.690430, Training Accuracy= 0.70312
Iter 10240, Minibatch Loss= 5066.223633, Training Accuracy= 0.70312 . . . .

     . . . . . . . . . . . . . . .
        . . . . . . . . . . . . . . . . . .
Iter 81920, Minibatch Loss= 442.895020, Training Accuracy= 0.93750
Iter 83200, Minibatch Loss= 273.936676, Training Accuracy= 0.93750
Iter 84480, Minibatch Loss= 1169.810303, Training Accuracy= 0.89062
Iter 85760, Minibatch Loss= 737.561157, Training Accuracy= 0.90625
Iter 87040, Minibatch Loss= 583.576965, Training Accuracy= 0.89844
Iter 88320, Minibatch Loss= 375.274475, Training Accuracy= 0.93750
Iter 89600, Minibatch Loss= 183.815613, Training Accuracy= 0.94531
Iter 90880, Minibatch Loss= 410.157867, Training Accuracy= 0.89844
Iter 92160, Minibatch Loss= 895.187683, Training Accuracy= 0.84375
Iter 93440, Minibatch Loss= 819.893555, Training Accuracy= 0.89062
Iter 94720, Minibatch Loss= 460.179779, Training Accuracy= 0.90625
Iter 96000, Minibatch Loss= 514.344482, Training Accuracy= 0.87500
Iter 97280, Minibatch Loss= 507.836975, Training Accuracy= 0.89844
Iter 98560, Minibatch Loss= 353.565735, Training Accuracy= 0.92188
Iter 99840, Minibatch Loss= 195.138626, Training Accuracy= 0.93750
Optimization Finished!
Testing Accuracy: 0.921875
```

It provides an accuracy of about 99.2%. Obviously, it does not represent the state of the art, because the purpose of the example is to just see how to build a CNN. The model can be further refined to give better results.

## Source code

```python
# Import MINST data
import input_data
mnist = input_data.read_data_sets("/tmp/data/",one_hot=True)
import tensorflow as tf
# Parameters
learning_rate = 0.001
training_iters = 100000
batch_size = 128
display_step = 10
# Network Parameters
n_input = 784 # MNIST data input (img shape: 28*28)
n_classes = 10 # MNIST total classes (0-9 digits)
dropout = 0.75 # Dropout, probability to keep units
# tf Graph input
x = tf.placeholder(tf.float32, [None, n_input])
y = tf.placeholder(tf.float32, [None, n_classes])
#dropout (keep probability)
keep_prob = tf.placeholder(tf.float32)
# Create model
def conv2d(img, w, b):
    return tf.nn.relu(tf.nn.bias_add\
                     (tf.nn.conv2d(img, w,\
                                   strides=[1, 1, 1, 1],\
                                   padding='SAME'),b))
def max_pool(img, k):
    return tf.nn.max_pool(img, \
                         ksize=[1, k, k, 1],\
                         strides=[1, k, k, 1],\
                         padding='SAME')
# Store layers weight & bias
# 5x5 conv, 1 input, 32 outputs
wc1 = tf.Variable(tf.random_normal([5, 5, 1, 32]))
bc1 = tf.Variable(tf.random_normal([32]))
# 5x5 conv, 32 inputs, 64 outputs
wc2 = tf.Variable(tf.random_normal([5, 5, 32, 64]))
bc2 = tf.Variable(tf.random_normal([64]))
# fully connected, 7*7*64 inputs, 1024 outputs
wd1 = tf.Variable(tf.random_normal([7*7*64, 1024]))
# 1024 inputs, 10 outputs (class prediction)
wout = tf.Variable(tf.random_normal([1024, n_classes]))
bd1 = tf.Variable(tf.random_normal([1024]))
```

```
bout = tf.Variable(tf.random_normal([n_classes]))
# Construct model
_X = tf.reshape(x, shape=[-1, 28, 28, 1])
# Convolution Layer
conv1 = conv2d(_X,wc1,bc1)
# Max Pooling (down-sampling)
conv1 = max_pool(conv1, k=2)
# Apply Dropout
conv1 = tf.nn.dropout(conv1,keep_prob)
# Convolution Layer
conv2 = conv2d(conv1,wc2,bc2)
# Max Pooling (down-sampling)
conv2 = max_pool(conv2, k=2)
# Apply Dropout
conv2 = tf.nn.dropout(conv2, keep_prob)
# Fully connected layer
# Reshape conv2 output to fit dense layer input
dense1 = tf.reshape(conv2, [-1, wd1.get_shape().as_list()[0]])
# Relu activation
dense1 = tf.nn.relu(tf.add(tf.matmul(dense1, wd1),bd1))
# Apply Dropout
dense1 = tf.nn.dropout(dense1, keep_prob)
# Output, class prediction
pred = tf.add(tf.matmul(dense1, wout), bout)
# Define loss and optimizer
cost = tf.reduce_mean\
(tf.nn.softmax_cross_entropy_with_logits(pred, y))
optimizer =\
        tf.train.AdamOptimizer\
(learning_rate=learning_rate).minimize(cost)
# Evaluate model
correct_pred = tf.equal(tf.argmax(pred,1), tf.argmax(y,1))
accuracy = tf.reduce_mean(tf.cast(correct_pred, tf.float32))
# Initializing the variables
init = tf.initialize_all_variables()
# Launch the graph
with tf.Session() as sess:
    sess.run(init)
    step = 1
    # Keep training until reach max iterations
    while step * batch_size < training_iters:
        batch_xs, batch_ys = mnist.train.next_batch(batch_size)
        # Fit training using batch data
        sess.run(optimizer, feed_dict={x: batch_xs,\
                                       y: batch_ys,\
                                       keep_prob: dropout})
        if step % display_step == 0:
            # Calculate batch accuracy
```

```
        acc = sess.run(accuracy, feed_dict={x: batch_xs,\
                                             y: batch_ys,\
                                             keep_prob: 1.})
        # Calculate batch loss
        loss = sess.run(cost, feed_dict={x: batch_xs,\
                                         y: batch_ys,\
                                         keep_prob: 1.})
        print "Iter " + str(step*batch_size) +\
              ", Minibatch Loss= " + \
              "{:.6f}".format(loss) + \
              ", Training Accuracy= " + \
              "{:.5f}".format(acc)
    step += 1
print "Optimization Finished!"
# Calculate accuracy for 256 mnist test images
print "Testing Accuracy:",\
    sess.run(accuracy,\
             feed_dict={x: mnist.test.images[:256], \
                        y: mnist.test.labels[:256],\
                        keep_prob: 1.})
```

# Recurrent neural networks

Another deep learning-oriented architecture is that of the so-called **recurrent neural networks (RNNs)**. The basic idea of RNNs is to make use of the *sequential information* type in the input. In neural networks, we typically assume that each input and output is independent from all the others. For many types of problems, however, this assumption does not result to be positive. For example, if you want to predict the next word of a phrase, it is certainly important to know those that precede it. These neural nets are called *recurrent* because they perform the same computations for all elements of a sequence of inputs, and the output each element depends, in addition to the current input, on all previous computations.

# RNN architecture

RNNs process a sequential input item at a time, maintaining a sort of *updated state vector* that contains information about *all past elements of the sequence*. In general, an RNN has a shape of the following type:

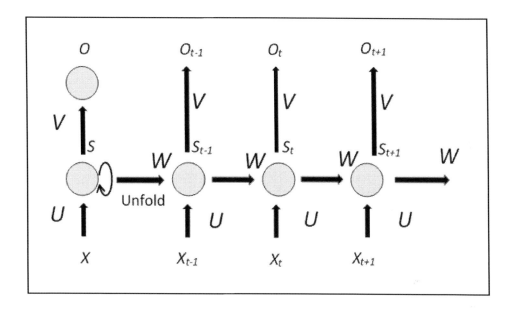

RNN architecture schema

The preceding figure shows the aspect of an RNN, with its *unfolded* version, explaining the network structure for the whole sequence of inputs, at each instant of time. It becomes clear that, differently from the typical multi-level neural networks, which *use several* parameters at *each level*, an RNN always uses *the same parameters*, denominated $U$, $V$, and $W$ (see the previous figure). Furthermore, an RNN performs the same computation at *each instant*, on *multiple of the same sequence in input*. Sharing the same parameters, it strongly reduces the number of parameters that the network must learn during the training phase, thus also improving the training time.

It is also evident how you can train networks of this type, in fact, because the parameters are *shared for each instant of time*, the gradient calculated for each output depends not only from the current computation but also from the previous ones. For example, to calculate the gradient at time $t = 4$, it is necessary to *back propagate* the gradient for the three previous instants of time and then sum the gradients thus obtained. Also, the *entire input sequence* is typically considered to be a *single element* of the training set.

However, the training of this type of network suffers from the so-called *vanishing/exploding gradient problem*; the gradients, computed and back propagated, tend to *increase* or *decrease* at each instant of time and then, after a certain number of instants of time, *diverge to infinity* or *converge to zero*.

Let us now examine how an RNN operates. $X_t$; is the network input at instant $t$, which could be, for example, a vector that represents a *word of a sentence*, while $S_t$; is the *state vector* of the net. It can be considered a sort of *memory* of the system which contains information on all the previous elements of the input sequence. The state vector at instant $t$ is evaluated starting from the *current input* (time $t$) and the *status* evaluated at the *previous instant* (time *t-1*) through the $U$ and $W$ parameters:

$$S_t = f\left([U]\, X_t + [W]\, S_{t-1}\right)$$

The function $f$ is a *non linear function* such as rectified linear unit (ReLu), while $O_t$; is the output at instant $t$, calculated using the parameter $V$.

The output will depend on the type of problem for the which the network is used. For example, if you want to predict the next word of a sentence, it could be a *probability vector* with respect to each word in the vocabulary of the system.

# LSTM networks

**Long Shared Term Memory** (**LSTM**) networks are an extension of the basic model of RNN architectures. The main idea is to improve the network, providing it with an explicit memory. The LSTM networks, in fact, despite not having an essentially different architecture from RNN, are equipped with special hidden units, called memory cells, the behavior of which is to remember the previous input for a long time.

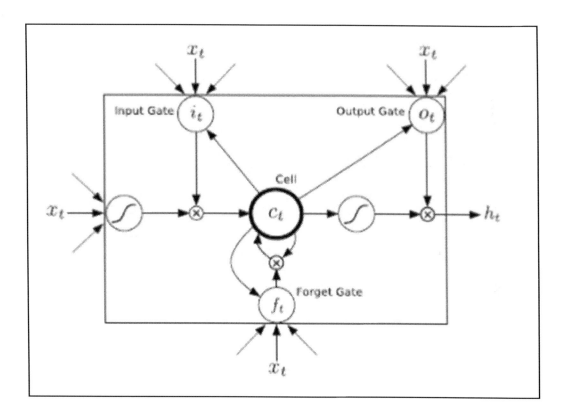

A LSTM) unit

The LSTM unit has three gates and four input weights, $xt$ (from the data to the input and three gates), while $ht$ is the output of the unit.

A LSTM block contains gates that determine whether an input is significant enough to be saved. This block is formed by four units:

- **Input gate**: Allows the value input in the structure
- **Forget gate**: Goes to eliminate the values contained in the structure
- **Output gate**: Determines when the unit will output the values trapped in structure
- **Cell**: Enables or disables the memory cell

In the next example, we will see a TensorFlow implementation of a LSTM network in a language processing problem.

# NLP with TensorFlow

RNNs have proved to have excellent performance in problems such as predicting the next character in a text or, similarly, the prediction of the next sequence word in a sentence. However, they are also used for more complex problems, such as **Machine Translation**. In this case, the network will have as input a sequence of words in a source language, while you want to output the corresponding sequence of words in a language *target*. Finally, another application of great importance in which RNNs are widely used is that of *speech recognition*. In the following, we will develop a computational model that can predict the next word in a text based on the sequence of the preceding words. To measure the *accuracy* of the model, we will use the **Penn Tree Bank** (**PTB**) dataset, which is the benchmark used to measure the precision of these models.

This example refers to the files that you find in the `/rnn/ptb` directory of your TensorFlow distribution. It comprises of the following two files:

- `ptb_word_lm.py`: The queues to train a language model on the PTB dataset
- `reader.py`: The code to read the dataset

Unlike previous examples, we will present only the pseudocode of the procedure implemented, in order to understand the main ideas behind the construction of the model, without getting bogged down in unnecessary implementation details. The source code is quite long, and an explanation of the code line by line would be too cumbersome.

See `https://www.tensorflow.org/versions/r0.8/tutorials/rec urrent/index.html` for other references.

## Download the data

You can download the data from the web page `http://www.fit.vutbr.cz/~imikolov/` `rnnlm/simple-examples.tgz` and then extract the data folder. The dataset is preprocessed and contains 10000, different words, including the end-of-sentence marker and a special symbol (`<unk>`) for rare words. We convert all of them in `reader.py` to unique integer identifiers to make it easy for the neural network to process.

To extract a `.tgz` file with tar, you need to use the following:

```
tar -xvzf /path/to/yourfile.tgz
```

# Building the model

This model implements an architecture of the RNN using the LSTM. In fact, it plans to increase the architecture of the RNN by including storage units that allow saving information regarding long-term temporal dependencies.

The TensorFlow library allows you to create a LSTM through the following command:

```
lstm = rnn_cell.BasicLSTMCell(size)
```

Here `size` should be the number of units to be used LSTM. The LSTM memory is initialized to zero:

```
state = tf.zeros([batch_size, lstm.state_size])
```

In the course of computation, after each word to examine the state value is updated with the output value, following is the pseudocode list of the implemented steps:

```
loss = 0.0
for current_batch_of_words in words_in_dataset:
        output, state = lstm(current_batch_of_words, state)
```

`output` is then used to make predictions on the prediction of the next word:

```
logits = tf.matmul(output, softmax_w) + softmax_b
probabilities = tf.nn.softmax(logits)
loss += loss_function(probabilities, target_words)
```

The `loss` function minimizes the average negative log probability of the target words, it is the TensorFow function:

```
tf.nn.seq2seq.sequence_loss_by_example
```

It computes the average per-word *perplexity*, its value measures the accuracy of the model (to lower values correspond best performance) and will be monitored throughout the training process.

# Running the code

The model implemented supports three types of configurations: small, medium, and large. The difference between them is in size of the LSTMs and the set of hyper parameters used for training. The larger the model, the better results it should get. The small model should be able to reach perplexity below 120 on the test set and the large one below 80, though it might take several hours to train.

To execute the model simply type the following:

```
python ptb_word_lm --data_path=/tmp/simple-examples/data/ --model small
```

In /tmp/simple-examples/data/, you must have downloaded the data from the PTB dataset.

The following list shows the run after 8 hours of training (13 epochs for a *small* configuration):

```
Epoch: 1 Learning rate: 1.000
0.004 perplexity: 5263.762 speed: 391 wps
0.104 perplexity: 837.607 speed: 429 wps
0.204 perplexity: 617.207 speed: 442 wps
0.304 perplexity: 498.160 speed: 438 wps
0.404 perplexity: 430.516 speed: 436 wps
0.504 perplexity: 386.339 speed: 427 wps
0.604 perplexity: 348.393 speed: 431 wps
0.703 perplexity: 322.351 speed: 432 wps
0.803 perplexity: 301.630 speed: 431 wps
0.903 perplexity: 282.417 speed: 434 wps
Epoch: 1 Train Perplexity: 268.124
Epoch: 1 Valid Perplexity: 180.210
Epoch: 2 Learning rate: 1.000
0.004 perplexity: 209.082 speed: 448 wps
0.104 perplexity: 150.589 speed: 437 wps
0.204 perplexity: 157.965 speed: 436 wps
0.304 perplexity: 152.896 speed: 453 wps
0.404 perplexity: 150.299 speed: 458 wps
0.504 perplexity: 147.984 speed: 462 wps
0.604 perplexity: 143.367 speed: 462 wps
0.703 perplexity: 141.246 speed: 446 wps
0.803 perplexity: 139.299 speed: 436 wps
```

```
0.903 perplexity: 135.632 speed: 435 wps
Epoch: 2 Train Perplexity: 133.576
Epoch: 2 Valid Perplexity: 143.072

. . . . . . . . . . . . . . . . . . . . . . . . . . . . . . . . . . . . . . . . . . . . . . . . . . .
Epoch: 12 Learning rate: 0.008
0.004 perplexity: 57.011 speed: 347 wps
0.104 perplexity: 41.305 speed: 356 wps
0.204 perplexity: 45.136 speed: 356 wps
0.304 perplexity: 43.386 speed: 357 wps
0.404 perplexity: 42.624 speed: 358 wps
0.504 perplexity: 41.980 speed: 358 wps
0.604 perplexity: 40.549 speed: 357 wps
0.703 perplexity: 39.943 speed: 357 wps
0.803 perplexity: 39.287 speed: 358 wps
0.903 perplexity: 37.949 speed: 359 wps
Epoch: 12 Train Perplexity: 37.125
Epoch: 12 Valid Perplexity: 123.571
Epoch: 13 Learning rate: 0.004
0.004 perplexity: 56.576 speed: 365 wps
0.104 perplexity: 40.989 speed: 358 wps
0.204 perplexity: 44.809 speed: 358 wps
0.304 perplexity: 43.082 speed: 356 wps
0.404 perplexity: 42.332 speed: 356 wps
0.504 perplexity: 41.694 speed: 356 wps
0.604 perplexity: 40.275 speed: 357 wps
0.703 perplexity: 39.673 speed: 356 wps
0.803 perplexity: 39.021 speed: 356 wps
0.903 perplexity: 37.690 speed: 356 wps
Epoch: 13 Train Perplexity: 36.869
Epoch: 13 Valid Perplexity: 123.358
Test Perplexity: 117.171
```

As you can see, the perplexity became lower after each epoch.

# Summary

In this chapter, we gave an overview of deep learning techniques, examining two of the deep learning architectures in use, CNN and RNNs. Through the TensorFlow library, we developed a convolutional neural network architecture for image classification problem. The last part of the chapter was devoted to RNNs, where we described the TensorFlow's tutorial for RNNs, where a LSTM network is built to predict the next word in an English sentence.

The next chapter shows the TensorFlow facilities for GPU computing and introduces *TensorFlow serving*, a high performance, open source serving system for machine learning models, designed for production environments and optimized for `TensorFlow`.

# 6
# GPU Programming and Serving with TensorFlow

In this chapter, we will cover the following topics:

- GPU programming
- TensorFlow Serving:
    - How to install TensorFlow Serving
    - How to use TensorFlow Serving
    - How to load and export a TensorFlow model

## GPU programming

In Chapter 5, *Deep Learning*, where we trained a **recurrent neural network** (**RNN**) for an NLP application, we could see that deep learning applications can be computationally intensive. However, you can reduce the training time by using parallel programming techniques through a **graphic processing unit** (**GPU**). In fact, the computational resources of modern graphics units make them able to perform parallel code portions, ensuring high performance.

The GPU programming model is a programming strategy that consists of replacing a CPU to a GPU to accelerate the execution of a variety of applications. The range of applications of this strategy is very large and is growing day by day; the GPUs, currently, are able to reduce the execution time of applications across different platforms, from cars to mobile phones, and from tablets to drones and robots.

The following diagram shows how the GPU programming model works. In the application, there are calls to tell the CPU to give away specific part of the code GPU and let it run to get high execution speed. The reason for such specific part to rely on two GPU is up to the speed provided by the GPU architecture. GPU has many **Streaming Multiprocessors (SMPs)**, with each having many computational cores. These cores are capable of performing ALU and other operations with the help of **Single Instruction Multiple Thread (SIMT)** calls, which reduce the execution time drastically.

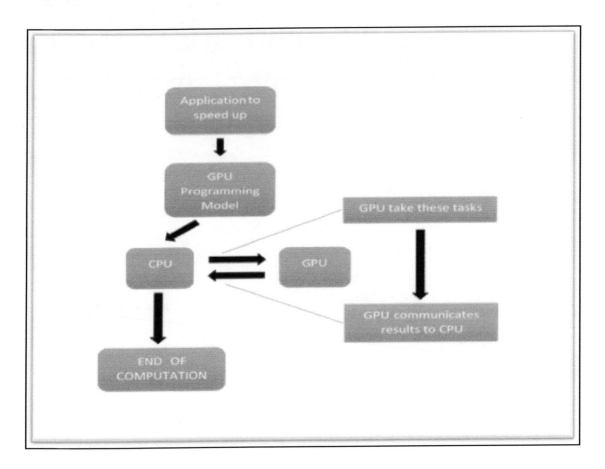

In the GPU programming model there are pieces of code that are executed sequentially in the CPU, and some parts are executed in parallel by the GPU

TensorFlow possesses capabilities that you can take advantage of this programming model (if you have a NVIDIA GPU), the package version that supports GPU requires Cuda Toolkit 7.0 and 6.5 CUDNN V2.

For the installation of Cuda environment, we suggest referring the Cuda installation page: `http://docs.nvidia.com/cuda/cuda-getting-sta rted-guide-for-linux/#axzz49w1XvzNj`

TensorFlow refers to these devices in the following way:

- `/cpu:0`: To reference the server CPU
- `/gpu:0`: The GPU server if there is only one
- `/gpu:1`: The second GPU server and so on

To find out which device is assigned to our operations and tensioners need to create the session with the option of setting `log_device_placement` instantiated to `True`.

Consider the following example.

We create a computational graph; a and b will be two matrices:

```
a = tf.constant([1.0, 2.0, 3.0, 4.0, 5.0, 6.0], shape=[2, 3], name='a')
b = tf.constant([1.0, 2.0, 3.0, 4.0, 5.0, 6.0], shape=[3, 2], name='b')
```

In c we put the matrix multiplication of these two input tensors:

```
c = tf.matmul(a, b)
```

Then we build a session with `log_device_placement` set to `True`:

```
sess = tf.Session(config=tf.ConfigProto(log_device_placement=True))
```

Finally, we launch the session:

```
print sess.run(c)
```

You should see the following output:

```
Device mapping:
/job:localhost/replica:0/task:0/gpu:0 -> device: 0, name: Tesla K40c,
pci bus
id: 0000:05:00.0
b: /job:localhost/replica:0/task:0/gpu:0
a: /job:localhost/replica:0/task:0/gpu:0
MatMul: /job:localhost/replica:0/task:0/gpu:0
[[ 22.   28.]
 [ 49.   64.]]
```

If you would like a particular operation to run on a device of your choice instead of what's automatically selected for you, you can use `tf.device` to create a device context, so that all the operations within that context will have the same device assignment.

Let's create the same computational graph using the `tf.device` instruction:

```
with tf.device('/cpu:0'):
    a = tf.constant([1.0, 2.0, 3.0, 4.0, 5.0, 6.0], shape=[2, 3], name='a')
    b = tf.constant([1.0, 2.0, 3.0, 4.0, 5.0, 6.0], shape=[3, 2], name='b')
    c = tf.matmul(a, b)
```

Again, we build the session graph and launch it:

```
sess = tf.Session(config=tf.ConfigProto(log_device_placement=True))
print sess.run(c)
```

You will see that now a and b are assigned to `cpu:0`:

```
Device mapping:
/job:localhost/replica:0/task:0/gpu:0 -> device: 0, name: Tesla K40c,
pci bus
id: 0000:05:00.0
b: /job:localhost/replica:0/task:0/cpu:0
a: /job:localhost/replica:0/task:0/cpu:0
MatMul: /job:localhost/replica:0/task:0/gpu:0
[[ 22.   28.]
 [ 49.   64.]]
```

If you have more than a GPU, you can directly select it setting `allow_soft_placement` to `True` in the configuration option when creating the session.

# TensorFlow Serving

Serving is a TensorFlow package that has been developed to take machine learning models into production systems. It means that a developer can use TensorFlow Serving's API to build a server to serve the implemented model.

The served model will be able to make inferences and predictions each time on data presented by its clients, allowing to improve the model.

To communicate with the serving system, the clients use a high performance open source **remote procedure call (RPC)** interface developed by Google, called gRPC.

The typical pipeline (see the following figure) is that training data is fed to the learner, which outputs a model. After being validated, it is ready to be deployed to the TensorFlow serving system. It is quite common to launch and iterate on our model over time, as new data becomes available, or as you improve the model.

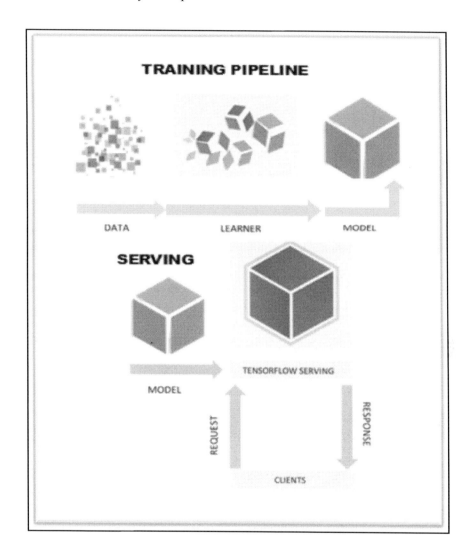

TensorFlow Serving pipeline

# How to install TensorFlow Serving

To compile and use TensorFlow Serving, you need to set up some prerequisites.

## Bazel

TensorFlow Serving requires Bazel 0.2.0 (`http://www.bazel.io/`) or higher. Download `bazel-0.2.0-installer-linux-x86_64.sh`.

Bazel is a tool that automates software builds and tests. Supported build tasks include running compilers and linkers to produce executable programs and libraries, and assembling deployable packages.

Run the following commands:

```
chmod +x bazel-0.2.0-installer-linux-x86_64.sh
./bazel-0.2.0-installer-linux-x86_64.sh --user
```

Finally, set up your environment. Export this in your `~/.bashrc` directory:

```
export PATH="$PATH:$HOME/bin"
```

## gRPC

Our tutorials use gRPC (0.13 or higher) as our RPC framework.

You can find other references at `https://github.com/grpc`.

### TensorFlow serving dependencies

To install TensorFlow serving dependencies, execute the following:

```
sudo apt-get update && sudo apt-get install -y \
        build-essential \
        curl \
        git \
        libfreetype6-dev \
        libpng12-dev \
        libzmq3-dev \
        pkg-config \
```

```
python-dev \
python-numpy \
python-pip \
software-properties-common \
swig \
zip \
zlib1g-dev
```

Then configure TensorFlow, by running the following command:

```
cd tensorflow
./configure
cd ..
```

## Install Serving

Use Git to clone the repository:

```
git clone --recurse-submodules
https://github.com/tensorflow/serving
cd serving
```

The `--recurse-submodules` option is required to fetch TensorFlow, gRPC, and other libraries that TensorFlow serving depends on. To build TensorFlow, you must use Bazel:

```
bazel build tensorflow_serving/
```

The binaries will be placed in the `bazel-bin` directory, and can be run using the following command:

```
/bazel-bin/tensorflow_serving/example/mnist_inference
```

Finally, you can test the installation by executing the following command:

```
bazel test tensorflow_serving/
```

# How to use TensorFlow Serving

In this tutorial, we will show how *to export* a trained TensorFlow model and *build a server* to serve the exported model. The implemented model is a Softmax Regression model for handwritten image classification (MNIST data).

The code will consist of two parts:

- A Python file (`mnist_export.py`) that trains and exports the model
- A C++ file (`mnist_inference.cc`) that loads the exported model and runs a gRPC service to serve it

In the following sections, we report the basic steps to use TensorFlow Serving. For other references, you can view `https://tensorflow.github.io/serving/serving_basic`.

# Training and exporting the TensorFlow model

As you can see in `mnist_export.py`, the training is done the same way as in the MNIST. For a beginners tutorial, refer the following link:

`https://www.tensorflow.org/versions/r0.9/tutorials/mnist/beginners/index.html`

The TensorFlow graph is launched in TensorFlow session `sess`, with the input tensor (image) as `x` and the output tensor (Softmax score) as `y`. Then we use the TensorFlow serving exporter to export the model; it builds a snapshot of the trained model so that it can be loaded later for inference. Let's now see the main function to use to export a trained model.

Import the `exporter` to serialize the model:

```
from tensorflow_serving.session_bundle import exporter
```

Then you must define `saver` using the TensorFlow function `tf.train.Saver`. It has the `sharded` parameter equal to `True`:

```
saver = tf.train.Saver(sharded=True)
```

`saver` is used to serialize graph variable values to the model export so that they can be properly restored later.

The next step is to define `model_exporter`:

```
model_exporter = exporter.Exporter(saver)
signature = exporter.classification_signature\
                    (input_tensor=x, scores_tensor=y)
model_exporter.init(sess.graph.as_graph_def(),
                default_graph_signature=signature)
```

`model_exporter` takes the following two arguments:

- `sess.graph.as_graph_def()` is the protobuf of the graph. Exporting will serialize the protobuf to the model export so that the TensorFlow graph can be properly restored later.
- `default_graph_signature=signature` specifies a model export signature. The signature specifies what type of model is being exported, and the input/output tensors to bind to when running inference. In this case, you use `exporter.classification_signature` to specify that the model is a classification model.

Finally, we create our `export`:

```
model_exporter.export(export_path,tf.constant\
                            (FLAGS.export_version), sess)
```

`model_exporter.export` takes the following arguments:

- `export_path` is the path of the export directory. Export will create the directory if it does not exist.
- `tf.constant(FLAGS.export_version)` is a tensor that specifies the version of the model. You should specify a larger integer value when exporting a newer version of the same model. Each version will be exported to a different sub-directory under the given path.
- `sess` is the TensorFlow session that holds the trained model you are exporting.

# Running a session

To export the model, first clear the export directory:

```
$>rm -rf /tmp/mnist_model
```

Then, using `bazel`, build the `mnist_export` example:

```
$>bazel build //tensorflow_serving/example:mnist_export
```

Finally, you can run the following example:

```
$>bazel-bin/tensorflow_serving/example/mnist_export /tmp/mnist_model
Training model...
Done training!
Exporting trained model to /tmp/mnist_model
Done exporting!
```

Looking in the export directory, we should have a sub-directory for exporting each version of the model:

```
$>ls /tmp/mnist_model
00000001
```

The corresponding sub-directory has the default value of 1, because we specified `tf.constant(FLAGS.export_version)` as the model version earlier, and `FLAGS.export_version` has the default value of 1.

Each version of sub-directory contains the following files:

- `export.meta` is the serialized `tensorflow::MetaGraphDef` of the model. It includes the graph definition of the model, as well as metadata of the model, such as signatures.
- `export-?????-of-?????` are files that hold the serialized variables of the graph.

```
$>ls /tmp/mnist_model/00000001
checkpoint export-00000-of-00001 export.meta
```

# Loading and exporting a TensorFlow model

The C++ code for loading the exportedTensorFlow model is in the `main()` function in `mnist_inference.cc`. Here we report an excerpt; we do not consider the parameters for batching. If you want to adjust the maximum batch size, timeout threshold, or the number of background threads used for batched inference, you can do so by setting more values in `BatchingParameters`:

```
int main(int argc, char** argv)
{
  SessionBundleConfig session_bundle_config;
          . . . Here batching parameters
  std::unique_ptr<SessionBundleFactory> bundle_factory;
  TF_QCHECK_OK(
      SessionBundleFactory::Create(session_bundle_config,
```

```
                                        &bundle_factory));
    std::unique_ptr<SessionBundle> bundle(new SessionBundle);
    TF_QCHECK_OK(bundle_factory->CreateSessionBundle(bundle_path,
                                        &bundle));

    ......
    RunServer(FLAGS_port, std::move(bundle));
    return 0;
}
```

`SessionBundle` is a component of TensorFlow Serving. Let's consider the include file `SessionBundle.h`:

```
struct SessionBundle {
  std::unique_ptr<tensorflow::Session> session;
  tensorflow::MetaGraphDef meta_graph_def;
};
```

The `session` parameter is a TensorFlow session that has the original graph with the necessary variables properly restored.

`SessionBundleFactory::CreateSessionBundle()` loads the exported TensorFlow model from `bundle_path` and creates a `SessionBundle` object for running inference with the model.

`RunServer` brings up a gRPC server that exports a single Classify() API.

Each inference request will be processed in the following steps:

1. Verify the input. The server expects exactly one MNIST-format image for each inference request.
2. Transform input to inference input tensor and create output tensor placeholder.
3. Run inference.

To run an inference, you must type the following command:

```
$>bazel build //tensorflow_serving/example:mnist_inference
$>bazel-bin/tensorflow_serving/example/mnist_inference --port=9000
/tmp/mnist_model/00000001
```

# Test the server

To test the server, we use the `mnist_client.py` (`https://github.com/tensorflow/serving/blob/master/tensorflow_serving/example/mnist_client.py`) utility.

This client downloads MNIST test data, sends it as requests to the server, and calculates the inference error rate.

To run it, type the following command:

```
$>bazel build //tensorflow_serving/example:mnist_client
$>bazel-bin/tensorflow_serving/example/mnist_client --num_tests=1000
--server=localhost:9000
Inference error rate: 10.5%
```

The result confirms that the server loads and runs the trained model successfully. In fact, a 10.5% inference error rate for 1,000 images gives us 91% accuracy for the trained Softmax model.

# Summary

We described two important features of TensorFlow in this chapter. First was the possibility of using the programming model known as *GPU computing*, with which it becomes possible to speed up the code (for example, the training phase of a neural network). The second part of the chapter was devoted to describing the framework *TensorFlow Serving*. It is a high performance, open source serving system for machine learning models, designed for production environments and optimized for TensorFlow. This powerful framework can run multiple models at large scale that change over time, based on real-world data, enabling a more efficient use of GPU resources and allowing the developer to improve their own machine learning models.

# Index

# U

# V

# W

Printed in Great Britain
by Amazon